When You Think God Isn't Fair

Staying Connected with God
after the Death of a Murdered Child

Dr. Sena Whitaker

Foreword by Presiding Prelate Bishop Jerry L. Maiden Sr.

XULON PRESS

Xulon Press
2301 Lucien Way #415
Maitland, FL 32751
407.339.4217
www.xulonpress.com

Unless otherwise indicated, Scripture quotations taken from the New King James Version (NKJV). Copyright © 1982 by Thomas Nelson, Inc. Used by permission. All rights reserved.

Unless otherwise indicated, Scripture quotations taken from the Holy Bible, New Living Translation (NLT). Copyright ©1996, 2004 by Tyndale House Foundation. Used by permission of Tyndale House Publishers, Inc.

Cover Design: Sena Whitaker, Tammie Mask, Xulon Press

Paperback ISBN-13: 978-1-6628-4585-7
Ebook ISBN-13: 978-1-6628-4586-4

Dedication

Omar Jamal Aycox
June 18, 1974
December 10, 1996

"For this child I prayed, and the Lord has granted me my petition which I asked of Him. Therefore, I also have lent him to the Lord; as long as he lives he shall be lent to the Lord..."

—*1 Samuel 1:27-28*

My Dearest Son:

I don't have the words to describe how deeply I miss you. Being your mom is one of the finest gifts God has ever given to me. My love for you is eternal, cannot be transferred to anyone else, and is more than most could ever believe.

Although you were only on earth for a brief 22 years, I am grateful for our time together. Your life was not an incomplete one. On the contrary, you brightened the lives of all who knew you and taught us that life consists not of duration but donation; it is not how long you live but the contribution you make that matters. Above all, you opened our minds to the realization that our time on earth is a vapor, and this world is not our home.

I look forward to the day when we will be together for eternity. But, until then, I have a longing ache for you that will live in my heart until we meet again.

Love,
"Mamas"

Silencing of the Prince

What can we say about a world of no love?
A land without respect
Children dying and mothers crying
Of homes filled with neglect.
What can we say about the needless pain?
This suffering makes no sense
Of the lion that used to roar so proud
Now the silencing of the Prince.
It seemed like only yesterday
We took you by the hand
Across the road of life's dismay
Through love, you became a man.
A heart that was blessed with faith and care
With a joyous soul inside
You took the steps that made us proud
And filled our lives with pride.
Yes, I remember you as a child
How quiet were your ways
How you always had that loving smile
On any given day.
But now your journey has started
And you didn't say so long
To the family that you loved so much
It was time to go back home.
Home to where the God you loved
To praise Him on the throne.
Do we say goodbye to Omar?
Now, we know that would be wrong
We bid farewell
We'll see you soon.
Omar, we say so long.
The Family
(Written by Anthony Jackson, Uncle)

Contents

Foreword

By
Bishop Jerry Maiden
Presiding Prelate of the National Assembly of the Church
of the Living God, PGT

J just finished reading a book written by Dr. Sena Whitaker that I just could not put down. I have known Dr. Whitaker and her husband, Pastor Earl Whitaker, for several years. But after reading her book concerning the fairness of God, I found an even greater respect and understanding of her anointed life.

In her book, "**When You <u>Think</u> God Isn't Fair**," she addresses an issue that is commonly felt although not commonly faced. Who among us have not at some time in our life felt that God was not being fair? Or how many of us have blamed God for allowing bad things to happen in our life? She very honestly and bravely opens to us her painful pathway back to trusting God after enduring the most horrific experience of her life, the death of her murdered son, Omar. She does a masterful job of expressing the **tragedy of her loss**.

In America gun violence is numbing. We are constantly reminded of its evil effects, not only to its victims but to their survivors as well. It is especially heartbreaking, when it happens to a young innocent, responsible and respectable person like Omar. Dr. Whitaker's story introduces us to her precious son, who in our estimation had so much to live for. But Omar was murdered, for no other reason than trying to do a good job. Then there is the

trial for her son's justice. Day by day having to go through court proceedings that can be brutal, reliving that awful day repeatedly, while at the same time sharing the same space with her son's murderer. Yet enduring the pain to seek justice for Omar who could not do it for himself.

Then there is the ***trust that seemed betrayed***; surely God will deal with her child's murderer in accordance with her hurt. Maybe now, God will rectify Himself and show *fairness* in the courtroom where there was none that night at the theatre where Omar was shot. How fragile our trust can be when we are hurting. The truth is revealed through Scripture. Jesus said, *"you shall know the truth and the truth shall make you free"* (John 8:32). It is not just the truth but *the truth that you know,* that leads you to ***trust regained in God.***

I recommend this book to all and especially those who may be struggling with the question of why or why not, as it relates to the *fairness* of God. Having lost my first wife without any warning, I was reminded of how I had some of the very same thoughts, feelings, and questions. Sena's story, although it may be different in experience, is very similar in expression as it relates to the spiritual and emotional existence of a Christian.

The word of God instructs us to *"Trust in the Lord with all thine heart and lean not to our own understanding. In all our ways acknowledge Him and He shall direct our path"* (Proverbs 3:5-6). The goal of our enemy (Satan) is to take advantage of these calamitous situations to sever our fellowship with God through doubt, disappointment, and disagreement. He works to draw us into measuring God by human standards and misunderstandings, even to the point of accusing God of the mismanagement of our affairs.

Have you misinterpreted God's will? Have you questioned God's love for you because He didn't do life the way you wanted? Has the enemy persuaded you into thinking you have been abandoned by God? Reconciliation, fellowship, and trust in God are vital to both our mental and moral stability. In this book you will see how God's strength is made perfect in our weakness. You will see the determination of a Believer who fights her way back through heartache to the loving arms of a faithful and just God. She shares with us the steps that she took to regaining, and transferring her trust from self, back to God. When you have finished reading this book, you should be able to say, if Sena can do it after all that she has gone through, I have hope.

God Bless you, Dr. Sena Whitaker, for letting God use your story for His glory.

Bishop Jerry L. Maiden, Sr. MTh.
Presiding Prelate of the National Assembly of The Church of the Living God, *The Pillar and Ground of the Truth,* Inc.
Graduate of United Theological Seminary and Bible College

In Gratitude

*A*bove all, I want to thank the triune and only living God: Father, Son, and Holy Spirit. I glorify You alone! Thank You for bringing Omar into my life for a brief stay, for guiding me in authoring this book from its inception to its completion, for compassionately listening to my heart, and for allowing me to live in the joy and confidence of Your unconditional love and care for me.

There are far too many people to thank individually. But some cannot go unmentioned:

My husband, Earl Whitaker Sr. For being more than a husband. You are my "knight in shining armor." Thank you for your love and friendship, for your interest and encouragement in the writing of my books, for your constructive feedback after reading the full manuscript of this book, and for letting God's love shine through you every day. I love and honor you.

Bishop Jerry Maiden. For your unique capacity to write the eloquent and touching Foreword from a heart that has experienced God's grace in the midst of consuming grief, and for giving me the inspiration for the title to this book from your mesmerizing sermon, "It's Not Fair!" I live with a profound sense of gratitude to you.

Amanda "Peggy" Young. For your invaluable suggestions and insights in refining the title of this book. I will always cherish you as one of my life's richest treasures.

Joseph Aycox Jr. (Jay). For being my special love, for being Omar's dearly beloved older brother, for being worth more to me than anything, for being the wind beneath my wings, and for reminding me repeatedly that "God is good!"

My amazing family. For your never-ending love and support. Special thanks to my siblings Elyse Wayns, Martha Brookings, Bertha "Bert" Jackson, and bonus sisters Thelma Kennedy-Malveaux and Evangelist Bernadine Ware. For standing with me through my triumphs, for walking me through my darkest nights, for giving me hope when things seemed hopeless, and for letting me lean on you during the grueling trials of Omar's murderers.

Marian Easley. For being Omar's other mother, for stealing his heart, for sharing my grief, and for your optimistic outlook on life.

Tammie Mask. For being my God-given bonus daughter, for loving Omar as a brother, though you never met him, for assisting with designing the cover and creating a Facebook page for my book.

Dr. Amanda Spencer. For your steadfast encouragement, enthusiasm, and goddaughter advice as I went through each writing stage, for helping me understand the process by which people overcome their heartbreak, and for funding the restoration of the photos on the covers and Dedication page of my book.

Presiding Bishop C. C. Berry, Jr, Sister Billie Berry, and The Church of the Living God, PGT. For your prayers, care, and comfort.

Bishop Jerry Burley. For spiritual insight and providing a steady hand when my world was crumbling.

William Dermott and coworkers at ExxonMobil. For your understanding and tenderness in the aftermath of Omar's death.

Chrissy Artes, Forever Studios, and Mark Chamberlain, Photograph Restoration. For restoring the photos included in my book.

Carmen Leano, Kristina Ross, and Federal Express Office #1858 staff. For binding numerous drafts of my book.

Kellie Lowrey and Antionette Osisanya, Office Depot #2387. For scanning the photos included in my book.

Xulon Press. For guidance in publishing my book.

Unnamed circle of friends. For being with me in my grief and beyond.

Thank you!
Sena

Author's Note

"Child loss is not an event; it's an indescribable journey of survival."
–Jessica Stanley LaPrade

The late Bishop Dr. Wheeler Jones preached a powerful sermon titled, "I've Been Through Enough Not to Know He's Enough." The message is on his Facebook page.[1] What makes it exceptionally powerful is that Bishop preached it amid Stage 4 cancer and a prognosis that he had less than six months to live. Nevertheless, his knowledge of God sustained him and gave him the strength to preach one of the most memorable sermons about God's love, grace, and mercy you can ever view and hear.

To know God this way can't come from someone else's story; it can only come from personal experience. That is why I had to author this book. Internal conflicts caused me to emotionally disconnect from God after the murder of my 22-year-old son, Omar, in 1996. As a result, I questioned God's fairness and made complex decisions regarding my relationship with Him.

My book is one that no one envisions reading. But, because you're reading it, there is a high probability that you or someone you know are grieving a child's death and are questioning God's justice. Or, you may have chosen my book to do a better job of comforting the bereaved who have lost a child. Finally, perhaps you selected this book because your life seems to be falling apart, and you are asking yourself, "Can I trust God in this situation?"

Though you didn't envision reading my book, thank you for choosing it. My goal is to provide you with a resource to encourage and comfort you as you move through your recovery process.

You may be asking, "Why did it take you 25 years to write about Omar's death?" The answer is simple—it didn't. I started journaling about Omar's death the day he died and continued to journal for 14 years. I also kept two small file cabinets of information relating to his death. But I just couldn't author a book about it. Every time I attempted to put my experience in a book, the emotions I felt that dreadful day when Omar died came flooding back to me, and the painful circumstances of his death were fresh to me again. And though 25 years have passed, I remember it as though it happened yesterday.

Tears are flowing down my face and dripping onto my T-shirt as I write this. But, as Ecclesiastes 3:1 says, "To everything there is a season and a time to every purpose under heaven." Now is the season, and now is the time to share my story with you. I thank God for giving me the strength to keep my files and journals open long enough to complete this book.

My book has also been therapeutic for me. Writing about my fickle, faltering, and faithless experiences took a lot of courage. But, at the same time, I want to assure you that my book is open and transparent. It doesn't contain pat answers, profound theology, or an over-simplification of the grief associated with the death of a child, and I do not hyper-spiritualize my feelings.

Finally, this book is a fulfillment of my promise to God. I promised Him if He would bring me through the most trying test of my life so far, I'd let the world know what He did. God loved me back to Him, so I must write about it.

Your Story

I don't know your story, but God does. He loves you, wants to heal you, and desires to have an intimate and thriving relationship with you. If you are willing to trust God and let Him lovingly have His way, He can use your journey as a stepping- stone to help others who are walking, or who will walk, along the pathway that leads to the death of a child or other devastating loss.

May you finish this book turning your heart toward God—even when you <u>think</u> He isn't fair.

Many blessings,
Sena

Introduction

"The Death of a Child
It's like losing your breath and never catching it again.
It's a forever panic attack as your soul is screaming for them.
It's a feeling your heart is dying as you continue to lose your mind."
—Unknown

$\mathcal{B}$efore I share my story with you, I'd like to take a few minutes to discuss perceived unfairness and the death of a child.

Perceived Unfairness

The supreme fulfillment in life is having an intimate connection with God. However, a close relationship with Him requires trust. If we perceive that God is unfair, it can cause us to distrust Him and break our connection with Him.

The Death of a Child

Few life events have the potential for disconnecting us from God like the death of our child. It is frequently called the ultimate tragedy.

Deborah Carr, chair of the sociology department at Boston University, says, "The death of a child is considered the single worst stressor a person can go through. Parents and fathers specifically feel responsible for the child's well-being. And they're not just losing a person they loved. They're also losing years of promises they had looked forward to."[2]

Homicide

Scores of children die by homicide. That is my personal experience. Murder is a horrendous death and the aftermath of murder is a tragic event.

The Compassionate Friends organization writes:

> *The death of a child of any age is devastating. The pain and anguish can be compounded when the death comes at the hands of another human being. Parents and family members can face many complicated issues, even as they try to make sense of the incomprehensible – that someone knowingly, willingly and/or intentionally killed their child.*[3]

Sadly, the murders of our children are increasing. All we have to do is pick up the daily newspaper or watch the news on TV to learn that this horrifying death is growing in number.

According to Statistica Research Department, the number of children murdered in the United States in 2019 was 4159. Age of victims in years was:

Infants less than 1- 154
1 to 4- 210
5 to 8- 116
9 to 12- 87
13-16- 307
17- 19- 1136
20-24- 2149[4]

Regardless of the circumstances surrounding our child's death, it hurts and seems so unjust of God to put us through insurmountable grief. The unquenchable throbbing seems beyond our capacity to survive. We all anticipate dying before our child; no one plans to make their child's funeral arrangements. We expect to see our children grow older and have grandchildren who look and act like them.[5]

Our child's death also seems inconsistent with God's love for us.

Questioning God

When we perceive that God isn't fair, it is natural to ask Him questions. Those relating to our child's death are perhaps the most complex we can ask. Correspondingly, answering our inquiries should not be an issue for a trustworthy God. But, sometimes, God does not respond to our questions. Unfortunately, when questions remain unanswered, they can cause us to withdraw from God and sever our intimacy with Him—leading to distrust, disappointment, discouragement, depression, and despair.

We can restore our connection with God by trusting Him with all our heart and not leaning on our understanding of His will, His way, and His Word (Proverbs 3:5-6).

Please join with me now as I share my healing journey with you.

AT FIRST

The Day My World Collapsed

"No farewell words were spoken,
no time to say goodbye; you were
gone before we knew it, and only
God knows why."
—Unknown

A Crisis

In his book *Letters to a Young Doctor*, Dr. Richard Seltzer writes:

Most of us seem to be protected for a time by an imaginary membrane that shields us from horror. We walk in and through it every day but are hardly aware of its presence. As the immune system protects the human body from the unseen threat of harmful bacteria, so this mythical membrane guards us from life-threatening situations. Not every young person has this protection, of course, because children do die of cancer, congenital heart problems, and other disorders. But most of them are shielded— and don't realize it. Then, as the years roll by, one day it happens. Without warning, the membrane tears and horror seeps into a person's life or into that of a loved one.

3

It is at this moment that an unexpected theological crisis presents itself.[6]

Robert Veninga identifies six characteristics of a crisis:

- First, a crisis hits suddenly, without warning, and it often strikes at a point in life in which everything is going well.
- Second, it threatens security.
- Third, its resolution is unpredictable; we don't know how things are going to turn out.
- Fourth, it presents dilemmas.
- Fifth, it erodes self-confidence.
- Sixth, it makes us redefine our values.[7]

Mega Crisis

Tuesday, December 10, 1996, God pulled His protective membrane from around me, and I faced the biggest crisis of my life, theological and otherwise. It had every one of the characteristics Mr. Veninga identified and more. It was the day someone murdered my son, Omar. The day my life changed in a blink of an eye. It was the day my world collapsed in an instant.

I didn't worship the Lord as Job did when his seven children were killed (Job 1:20), or say as he said in Job 2:10, "Shall we accept good from God and shall we not accept adversity?" And I didn't say, "It is well," like the Shunammite woman did in 2 Kings 4:23. But I could relate to what Job said in Job 17:7—"My eyes have grown dim with grief; my whole frame is but a shadow." I thought I was going to lose my mind!

It was ironic that Omar was pronounced dead shortly after the darkest hour of the night—1:14 a.m. As Dr. David Jeremiah said, "The darkness of the night depends on the moon, stars, clouds, and weather patterns. All things being equal, the sky is blackest when the sun is aligned 180 degrees from our position on earth, which is midnight.[8]

Breaking News

I didn't know about Omar's death until my former husband, Joel (1942-2001), watched the morning news, and a Breaking News story interrupted the programming: There had been a murder at the AMC theater at Interstate 45 and Richey Road, Houston, Texas, which was the theater where Omar worked. Joel went to Omar's bedroom to check on him. He woke me up when Omar wasn't there. That was unusual because Omar always came home after work. I thought he may have stopped by his girlfriend Olivia's house before going home. We called Olivia, and she told us he wasn't there.

Joel and I decided to go to the theater. Maybe Omar had to work late since he would start managing the theater Wednesday, after a day of vacation. When we arrived at the theater, I saw Omar's small gray rental car in the parking lot, and in my heart, I knew Omar was dead. So I went inside the theater and asked the Assistant Manager three questions: (1) Was there a murder at the theater last night? (2) Was a young man killed? (3) Was the young man named Omar?" He answered "Yes" to each of the questions.

Severe Shock

I didn't know what to do. I was in severe shock and started hyperventilating. I have never had such a feeling of helplessness. Then, dazed, I asked God, "*Father, how could you let this happen? Why? Why? Why?*" The stabbing emotional hurt was so intense that I could hardly breathe; it was too appalling for my mind to absorb. Life as I knew it stopped. It turned upside down. I bolted out the front door of the theater and ran down the parking lot crying uncontrollably and screaming inside, trying to push the thought out of my mind that Omar was dead. I kept running until Joel caught up with me.

I was confused, and my mind blurred as we walked back to the theater and asked the day manager what had happened. He said the night manager and Omar were closing for the night, and she noticed that the lights were on in the back of the theater. Omar volunteered to turn them off, and two robbers confronted him. One of them shot him in the back four times. Omar made it to the theater's lobby and died on the floor.

Joel and I drove back home after talking with the manager. I felt like I had an out-of-body experience. I couldn't believe Omar was dead. Violence wasn't part of my life, and I couldn't accept it. Murder happens on TV, not to my child. How could a young, vibrant young man be alive one moment and dead the next? *How could this happen to Omar? To my baby?*

Thrown into a Tailspin

As a minister, I was familiar with death, and I had buried loved ones of my own. I delivered the eulogy for my beloved mother in 1989. But Omar's death threw me into a tailspin. My soul was troubled when we arrived home, and my grief was bottomless. I couldn't put a name to what I was feeling. I was so puzzled by what had transpired.

I didn't have time to prepare for his sudden, unexpected death. I didn't even have a warning. I didn't have a chance to say goodbye and tell him I loved him. If Omar had died from an illness or an accident, I felt I would have been able to accept that. I could have been there and spent the last moments of his life with him if God had decided not to intervene. I could have kissed him and painfully said goodbye. If I weren't there, someone would have been at his side to record the exact time he passed away. So why didn't God just let him slip away? Why murder?

Calls I Didn't Want to Make

I was in an automatic response mode, and my mind was on autopilot. But I had to make critical phone calls to my family, Olivia, and my late Pastor, Bishop Ural Ware, to tell them that Omar was dead. Their hysterical responses were nerve-wracking. Finally, I called my office to tell my manager, Bill Dermott, that I would not be coming to work that day, nor knew when I would return. Then, one of my team members gave me her condolences and said she would let the rest of my coworkers know about Omar's death.

It wasn't long before calls from my friends and coworkers started pouring in. So many of them came to our home. At times there were no words. We could only embrace one another and cry together.

Public Intrusion

Since Omar was murdered, our life was open to public intrusion—the police and the media.

Thanks to God, the police didn't knock on my door at 3:00 a.m. to tell me that Omar was dead. Our address was on his license, but they didn't come to our home for some reason. Later, we found out they tried to reach us by calling Omar's number, but we didn't hear his phone ringing. That's why we didn't know anything until Joel heard about it on the news.

Nevertheless, Joel and I had endless questions from two detectives who arrived at our home that afternoon. They explained what had transpired and interrogated us about our relationship with Omar. They also probed into our business and asked us how much insurance we had on Omar. I didn't want to talk about anything. Despite that, they had to ask the questions as many murders are perpetrated by those closest to the victim. That was not the case here!

Reporters also called and asked to interview Joel and me. A couple of them came to our home; a few met us at the funeral home the next day. I gave each of them one of Omar's graduation photos. In addition, our local news channel featured the story of Omar's murder on the evening news that night (It was broadcast 20 times between December 10th and 13th on each of the news channels and reported in our local newspaper several times).

Sleepless Night

It was a long day. Before going to bed, I dropped down on my knees to pray to God. It was so hard. I couldn't find any words; all I did was cry into the pillow. *God, I'm hurting and need Your comfort!*

I was wiped out, mentally anguished, and locked down in my thoughts when I got into the bed. And I couldn't sleep. I thought about the day Omar and I were riding to church, and he asked me the root word for funeral. I didn't know. He said, "Mom, it's fun. When I die, I want my funeral to be fun." This thought was alarming, and I tried to get it out of my mind.

I also reflected on how the Holy Spirit spoke to my spirit shortly before Thanksgiving. I was ministering after our group, Singers of Joy, had finished singing, "He's an On-Time God." The Holy Spirit asked me, "How do you know He's an on-time God?" Then He said, "You don't know now, but you will know." *Was He referring to Omar's death?*

In addition, I spent time reflecting on the morning and night before Omar's death. That night, Joel and I decided to go Christmas shopping. Joel suggested stopping by the theater to see Omar. I said, "No. Omar doesn't want his parents to show up at his job," so we didn't go. How I dread that decision!

But most of the night, I lay in bed traumatized and thinking about the events leading up to Omar's unthinkable and irreversible death. I had disturbing images of his last minutes. Did he call out to God? Did he call out to me? How long did he suffer? Did he know he was going to die? Why didn't God intervene? I knew He was present everywhere, was all-knowing, and all-powerful. So why didn't He direct the bullet away from Omar's vital organs? I couldn't come to grips with it.

I tried to control Omar's safety. I kept him close and was a strict parent. When he started working at AMC, I insisted that he take a safer route with well-lit streets on the way home from work, even though he preferred the quick, dark ones. I made him promise that he would take the longer, safer route. He'd simply say, *"Mamas, I'm fine. You don't have to worry about me."* Wrong! I never thought about danger at the theater.

Instead of going to sleep, I got out one of my new journals and started writing about the day's events. I've always enjoyed writing and journaling, and it helped relieve the aching I was experiencing.

By God's grace, I went to sleep in the wee hours of Wednesday morning, December 11, 1996, and had the dream I write about in my chapter, *Dreams and Nightmares.*

Goodbye To Yesterday

"Goodbyes hurt the most when the story was not finished."
–Jennifer Cindric

When someone dies, all your memories of them are in the past. It's no different when you lose a child; they are all yesterday. And there comes a time when you have to say goodbye to yesterday. I'm talking about homegoing, funeral, or memorial services.

Preparing for the Services

We had to plan a wake and two homegoing services. How? Quickly! Gratefully, I had plenty of help.

Wednesday, December 11, Bishop Ware and his wife, Evangelist Bernadine Ware, met Joel and me at Carl Barnes' Funeral Home to plan for Omar's services. We selected a blue casket, and I wanted Omar dressed in one of the new suits I purchased for him for Christmas as part of his wardrobe as the new manager at AMC.

My sisters, Elyse and Martha, arrived from Philadelphia Wednesday afternoon. They drafted the Order of Service with Thelma, my bonus sister in Texas. Martha took the lead in writing the obituary. She did a phenomenal job describing *"The Legacy of Omar Jamal Aycox."* She started Omar's legacy with, "In the summer of 1974, a bud became a flower on a big, old oak tree. The tree had been standing for years and decided to blossom on June 18." She closed with: "On December 10, 1996, during the fall of 1996, our flower closed his beautiful brown eyes. Like other precious flowers, life was too short."

Viewing Omar's Body

Thursday, December 12, Joel, my sisters, and I went to the funeral home to view Omar's body for the first time. As we drove there, I was so weak and light-headed that I thought I would pass out.

When we arrived at the funeral home, I slowly walked up to the casket, wondering how Omar's body would look. Unlike so many others who've had loved ones murdered, Omar's body wasn't beaten, dismembered, or burned to destroy evidence of his murder. But I didn't know what to expect because I had heard that being shot often alters the body's appearance so much that you can hardly recognize the deceased. And, at a minimum, I could expect his body to be bloated.

Omar was trim, so I dreaded viewing a distorted and bloated body. God's grace prevailed. The morticians at Carl Barnes' Funeral Home did a magnificent job. Omar looked like he was—a handsome, young man who had just fallen asleep.

I was so relieved as I had been contemplating whether to have the casket open or closed. We kept it open. I placed a black stuffed dog in it to represent Omar's love for animals.

Wake

The wake was held at 6 p.m. Thursday at our church, The Church of the Living God, Temple #18. The service was packed, and my private grief became public due to the nature of Omar's death. Total strangers came to view his body. Police officers and the media stood outside of the church during the wake.

I acted joyfully and wore a red suit (Omar's favorite color) at the wake so my friends would think I had joy, but I didn't feel joyful by any stretch of the imagination. And yet, God gave me the strength to shake hands with everyone. He also gave me the ability to go to the microphone and assure my family and friends that I had the power to deliver the eulogy the following day.

Homegoing Service in Houston

We held Omar's homegoing service Friday, December 13, at 11:00 a.m. in the Williams Temple Church of God in Christ, Houston, TX. Bishop Ware officiated, and I delivered the eulogy.

The program read, "In Celebration of Life." It was an ideal service and very well attended. Even in death, Omar had a heartfelt impact on the lives he touched. He had only lived in Houston four months after returning from college and didn't hang out with many people, so I was somewhat surprised by the turnout. A few Morehouse Alumni attended. One gave a tribute to Omar during the services.

My subject for Omar's eulogy was "Our Enemy is Already Defeated." The Scripture text was 2 Samuel 5:17-25. It was the message that God gave me before Omar's death. I was scheduled to preach it the Sunday after Thanksgiving but preached another message instead.

My message centered on how death was a defeated enemy, and we were victorious through Christ. It was a faith-strengthening message that brought words of life and hope to others while hiding my discomfort. I believed every word I preached, but I was heartbroken. Omar was a Christian, so I didn't have to worry about where he was. He was in heaven. He rededicated his life to God the day before he died, so his eternal destination was not an issue. Still, it hurt so badly! That was my baby!

When I finished the eulogy, I stood next to the casket and shook hands with my friends to comfort them as they viewed Omar's body. I knew they were looking to me for strength.

Homegoing Service in Philadelphia

We had a private second homegoing service in my hometown of Philadelphia, Pennsylvania, for relatives and close family friends. It was held Wednesday, December 18, at 10:30 a.m. in the Antioch Baptist Church. The program read, "Graduation to Glory Services." Joel officiated, and I delivered the eulogy. My message was "There is Hope," text: 1 Thessalonians 4:13-18. It was an upbeat, non-traditional service. My nephew, Andrez, played CDs. Yolanda Adam's song, "The Battle is the Lord's," especially ministered to me because that was the song my sister Elyse and I listened to all night long the day she arrived in Texas after hearing about Omar's death.

After the message, I gave an invitation to accept Christ, and many of my family members responded. I said to God, "I didn't want my son to die so they could be saved." I remember hearing God saying, "My Son died so you could be saved."

The last item on the program was a Song of Triumph— "Shake the Devil Off."

Burial

Joel and I buried Omar in Forest Hills Cemetery in a plot close to my parents and we purchased a double marker with Omar's and Jay's names. Under Omar's name are the words, "Our Conqueror."

Burying Omar was one of the most frightful parts of my grief. Here's an excerpt from my book, *I'm Sleeping With the Pastor!!!* I can never ever adequately express how I felt when I committed his body to the ground:

As I stood over the silvery blue casket and pronounced the words, "Earth to earth, ashes to ashes and dust to dust," a million memories rushed through my head like a powerful water stream about the young man whose body we were laying to rest.

Memories of the times I lay on the bed with him listening to his dreams before and after he graduated from Morehouse College in Atlanta, Georgia. Or just talking about his day, and what he and his girlfriend Olivia were planning to do. Or laughing at one of the jokes that he always seemed to have ready for those who needed something to cheer their day. I even thought back to his simultaneous first and last recital. I wanted him to play the piano; he wanted to play the sax. I thought about how he wanted to be a comedian and a lawyer; I wanted him to be a lawyer first and then a comedian.

As my thoughts raced on like a skier going downhill, I thought about his first steps and his first words. I even thought about the nine months I had carried him in my womb, and the joy he brought to my life and the life of others in so many ways. What was I doing at his gravesite after only twenty-two years of life?

When I said goodbye to him on December 9, 1996, I couldn't have known that would be the last time I would lay eyes on him. He was killed on his job by armed robbers. Shot four times in the back. The coroner was called to the scene, and at 1:14 a.m., he was pronounced "Dead On Arrival." So here I was saying, "Earth to earth, dust to dust, ashes to ashes.[9]

Repast

After the internment, we had a repast with family and friends at my sister Bert's home. I slowly drifted most of the time, and I didn't shake the devil off. Instead, I focused on the fact that Omar's body was in that cold ground.

Visits to the Gravesite

Joel and I visited Omar's gravesite several times before going back to Texas.

Each time we visited, I would mourn and open my heart to God, begging Him to bring Omar back. Finally, I felt if God wasn't going to grant my request, the least I could do was make Omar more comfortable. The vault surrounding his casket was concrete because that's what Pennsylvania required. But now, that wasn't good enough. I wanted to have his body dug up and placed in a much more expensive vault.

I discussed this with my sister, Elyse, and she questioned my faith. If I believed Omar was in heaven, why would I want to do this? So I decided against upgrading the vault.

A Glimpse of "The Prince"

"I carried you every second of your life, and I will love you every second of mine."
–Jessica Urbina

The Prince

*I*f you were to Google "Bill Cosby's Son Murdered," you will find numerous articles and TV documentaries on the death of William Ennis Cosby, who was tragically murdered on January 17, 1997, while changing the tire on his Mercedes Benz. From all accounts, he appeared to be a fine young man. As God ordained, Omar was not born to celebrity parents, and the world doesn't know what a fine young man it lost when he died. I could fill this book writing about how blessed I was to have Omar for a son. Instead, I hope this chapter will help you get to know him a little.

My nickname for Omar was "Flash" because he was never in a hurry. For this chapter, I'll borrow from what my brother Anthony called him— "The Prince."

Omar wrote on his application for admittance to Morehouse College:

I describe myself as a shy but intelligent person who has a great sense of humor. I am likable, and I have a nice personality. I am now trying to eliminate my shyness. I feel that I would meet more people and accomplish more goals if I weren't so shy....

...I see myself as an interested observer. I often sit in the background and listen to what's being said, but I hope to become a leader because I think I would function better as a leader.

I agree with everything Omar wrote about himself. But there is so much more to Omar than being a shy, intelligent young man who hoped to become a leader. I have no illusions about his imperfections, but he was the child any mother would want to have.

I'm Pregnant!

My relationship with Omar began as soon as I found out I was pregnant. When my obstetrician told me I was having another boy, I didn't have to consult baby books or ask family members about a potential name—I always wanted a little boy named Omar. I considered giving that name to my oldest son, Jay. But, instead, we named him Joseph Jr. after his father. I selected Jamal as Omar's middle name because I liked Ahmad Jamal, the musician.

My relationship with Omar grew when I felt the first flutter inside my body. It became closer when he kicked or moved inside my womb. I lived with him for nine months with the expectancy that he would bring much joy to my life. He did.

My closeness to Omar increased after he was born. On June 18, 1974, He entered my life as a 6-lb, 14 oz bundle of joy. He was a beautiful baby, and I loved to show him off. I dedicated Omar to God when he was six God when he was six months old. He was christened in his little white outfit with the cute cap, as his godparents, Sally and George Conley, held him. We had a big celebration afterward at their home.

Elementary School

Omar was a straight "A" student in elementary school and received many awards, though we had different goals for music and sports. I wanted him to play the piano, so I enrolled him in the school's music program. He played one verse of Frere Jacques at his recital, took a bow, and sat down. That was the last time he played the piano.

He also played soccer in elementary school but didn't want to continue.

High School

Omar was a typical teenager with usual adolescent problems. Even so, I watched with pride as he grew into a quiet, caring, intelligent, easy-tempered, quick-witted, fun-loving, well-mannered, Christian young man with character.

He excelled academically in junior and senior high school and filled our home with awards and commendations he received for his academic ability. But Omar wasn't much for studying. He didn't have to; he was intellectually gifted, so I had to stay on his case to turn the TV off. When he did, he aced his homework, drafted beautiful essays, and would get better grades on exams after studying for two hours than I would have obtained after studying two weeks.

Additionally, Omar played football during his first year in junior high school but wasn't interested in continuing. In high school, he excelled in playing the alto sax and was the first chair for the two years he played in the orchestra but decided it was not his passion.

Friendships

Omar's life was rich in friendships. The characteristic everyone noticed and what he emanated was love. One of our neighbors fell in love with him shortly after he was born. She wanted to keep him every weekend for free, and he often stayed at her home. When she grew too attached, I knew it was time to reclaim my baby. He also stole the teacher's heart when he attended Head Start and often spent time with her on the weekends. After that, he was the "teacher's pet" in just about every grade he attended.

The children even loved Omar. I'm sure part of their love for him was because of his laid-back personality. He was a real kid at heart, and nothing seemed to bother him. Whenever I think of when he took the children from church to McDonald's, it brings a smile to my face. He got into a minor fender bender and was terrified when he returned to the church. I assured him that it was okay.

Pet Lover

Omar also loved pets and always had a dog, though he wasn't too crazy about walking them. He had to drag one of his dogs, Bo, down the street because he had gotten so used to being carried. Omar couldn't take Bo to college, so he bought a hamster. He also wanted a snake but decided against it.

Vocational Interests

Omar was interested in veterinarian medicine and becoming a lawyer—often referring to himself as Omar Aycox, Esq. However, his life-long desire was to become a comedian. He was a natural and made us laugh from the time he was able to talk. He would always do something crazy—like putting a plastic ice cube with a spider in his Grandmom's glass and laughing while she tried to determine how it got there.

Shortly before he died, he was practicing his comedy routine as an opening for Julie Johnson, my friend who is a singer. I shared his dreams but encouraged him to get a good education before pursuing his passion for being a comedian. He decided that he no longer wanted to be a lawyer and chose International

Business because he wanted to have an international office cleaning company.

Personal Note

On a more personal note, Omar called me Mom, but his term of endearment for me was "Mamas." He usually called me that when we were joking around or he was trying to get my attention. When he got it, he talked to me about everything—including private matters that I wish he had kept to himself!

And, when I preached, he would sink into the pew as though he was unconcerned. I would get so upset with him; he should have set an example by being attentive. But he would tell me every point of my message when I questioned him about what I said.

I have fond memories of when we would go to the store, and he would put limits on my spending. He thought I was too extravagant at times. I had to remind him that I was his mother!

Morehouse College

Omar received full-tuition scholarships from several colleges and a National Merit scholarship. Indeed, one of my highest joys was when he received a four-year Morehouse Scholars Programs academic scholarship to attend Morehouse College in Atlanta, GA, an institution known for developing Black leaders.

When I visited him on campus, I was awed by the change that was taking place in him as he grew from a boy into a Morehouse Man. He was more disciplined about studying. He even gave his TV to his girlfriend, Olivia, to stay focused on his studies.

Omar's time at Morehouse wasn't all peaches and cream. One of his professors called me and told me that Omar was brilliant and asked such insightful and probing questions that he had to research the answers. Despite this, Omar seemed reluctant to display his intelligence because he didn't want to be labeled a "nerd."

So I called Omar and had a "you'd better get yourself together real quick" conversation with him.

Things changed during Omar's senior year at Morehouse. He overcame his shyness and had grown into a confident Morehouse young man full of dreams and aspirations—one who had the world by the tail. He even started to look differently—had a slight beard and a mustache, which he wore well. Yet, for all that, he was not self-seeking or conceited. In contrast, Omar was his own worst critic. I welcomed the transition and was glad that he never lost his sense of humor, compassion, or gentleness. I was also pleased that he started to dress a little more upscale—though he preferred to wear jeans.

Omar graduated from Morehouse on May 19, 1996, with a Bachelor of Arts degree in Business Administration, majoring in Marketing. After graduating, he stayed in Georgia for several months, working as a Resident Assistant at Florida A&M, then returned home to work before continuing his education.

After College

Omar planned to attend the University of Texas at Austin (UTA), majoring in International Business. However, UTA required students with no business experience to work a minimum of one year before enrolling in the MBA program. Therefore, Omar decided to get a job to gain business experience and to join the Air Force Reserve.

He passed the Air Force test with flying colors, but he wasn't ready to make a two-year commitment. But, he enjoyed the movies, so I wasn't surprised when he decided to take a job at AMC in the general management program. Omar advanced through the training program rapidly. He did so well in the manager-trainee program that he completed the program in six weeks. The general manager said it took her a few months to complete. Of course, he had to dress up: navy blue sports jacket, light blue shirt, and gray slacks. I was so proud of him!

God Answered My Prayers

I thanked God daily for Omar as I did for my son, Jay. I prayed for God to protect them and allow me to live to see both of them grown.

God answered my prayers. He spared Omar's life so many times. For instance, when Omar was about nine months old, he started to swell up for no reason and ended up in the hospital in a plastic bubble to protect him from infection. The doctors didn't know what was wrong with him. My sister, Elyse, knew an Evangelist who had a prayer ministry. She came to the hospital to pray for Omar. He was sitting up in a couple of days and released from the hospital a few days later. I had faith that God would continue to protect him. He did.

Another time, when he was about three years old, I was at the table playing cards with my family. Omar was on my lap and wanted to get down. He got hold of scissors and tried to cut the cord to the TV while it was on. He brought burned scissors to me, but God spared him.

I believed that God would continue to spare Omar's life and allow him to live a long life. This was particularly important to me as Jay had an intellectual disability and could not live independently. I knew Omar loved him and would give him the best care possible after my death.

The Days Before He Died

Sunday, December 8th, after church, Joel, Omar, and I went out to eat. Omar and I ordered his favorite meal: shrimp, fries, salad with ranch dressing, and cheesecake. Joel was upset at all the food we ordered. We just laughed and enjoyed lunch together.

Monday, December 9th, Omar was scheduled to work from 3 p.m. to 11 p.m. I stopped by his room that morning before I went to work. He was in a light mood and told me he had received a jury duty summons. I told him, welcome to the real world. Then he smiled and said that the manager would give him the keys that night. He would take a day of vacation, then be the manager. He was excited, and I was too. We were both flying on the red carpet. I kissed him on the forehead and told him I loved him and that I'd see him when he returned home after work.

I never did—at least not alive.

No, Omar wasn't perfect, but he certainly was a Prince!

Oh, how I miss my Baby!

Coping with the Holidays

"You will always be the first thing I think of when someone says, Make a Wish."
—*Unknown*

The First Holidays

The first holidays after Omar's death, Christmas, 1996, and New Year, 1997, were very tough for me. He died 15 days before Christmas and 22 days before New Year. After Omar's funeral, I decided to stay in Philadelphia and share Christmas with my family. At the same time, it was unthinkable that I would enjoy the holidays, and I felt anything but festive when they came.

Joel and I went shopping for Jay and other family members as Christmas approached, though I was on edge. It was distressing to look at the enormous real Christmas tree in the mall. I thought about how Omar would have liked the brightly decorated tree. He disliked anything artificial—trees, flowers, and dolls. When he was alive, we always had a real tree. End of discussion!

Additionally, I didn't want to hear someone tell me, "Merry Christmas." My Christmas wasn't going to be merry. It was much too soon for that! Yet, I found myself caught between grief and obligations because I knew how important it was to celebrate Christmas. It is the day we Christians commemorate the birth of our Lord and Savior, Jesus Christ.

Thankfully, I made it through Christmas and returned home to Texas. But, in the same fashion, I didn't want anyone to tell me, "Happy New Year." My new year wasn't going to be happy, and I wasn't optimistic about a future without Omar. But God's grace strengthened me to make it through the New Year without going wild.

I also received a special after New Year surprise. On January 3, 1997, my sister Thelma visited our home with my two young nieces, Phaziah and Qadara. The children brightened up my day with a mini-concert. They also gave me a figurine of a young male angel patting a dog. I couldn't keep from crying and thanking God for the joy Thelma and my nieces brought to me that day. The figurine also prompted me to start the collection of memories of Omar I mentioned in the chapter, *Savoring Memories*.

Midnight Plane to Georgia

"I was supposed to protect you forever. I was supposed to guide, teach, and love you forever. I was NOT supposed to miss you forever."
–Vicki Loree

*G*ladys Knight and the Pips recorded a song, *Midnight Train to Georgia*. The song is about a man from Georgia who couldn't make it in Los Angeles (LA), so he's leaving LA to return to Georgia. The woman who loves him is going with him on the train because she'd rather live in Georgia than without him in LA. It was a difficult decision, but love made her do it.

A Different Kind of Trip

Thursday, January 9, 1997, I took a different kind of trip to Georgia. I didn't go on a train; I flew. According to the watch on my wrist, it wasn't midnight, but it was midnight in my heart. The trip was the worse flight I had taken to Georgia during the four years Omar attended Morehouse. Love made me do it.

Previously, I enjoyed each trip Joel and I took. Omar would show us new things on campus and take us to "old-fashioned" diners that served giant hamburgers and chocolate shakes. I went to Georgia this time to move Omar's belongings out of storage to Cypress, Texas, where we lived. Omar graduated in May 1996, and the rental on his storage unit expired on December 31st. He intended to return to Georgia before then and clean out his storage facility.

The thought of going through Omar's belongings was awful. I wanted to hang on to everything that belonged to him. Occasionally, I would sit on his bed, smell the scent in his clothes at home, hold them close to me and cry. So, I asked Joel to pack his things when we got to Georgia. Surprisingly, when we got to the storage facility, I saw that Omar had already packed many of his items. Joel packed the rest, and I wrapped his photos and paintings.

Ah! I can hardly write this! The memories are so vivid!

Returning to Cypress

After packing, we took the flight back home on Friday, January 11, 1997. Omar had a large framed painting I sent to him that I wanted to carry on the plane. It was of a mother washing a baby about six months old in a tub. I told him always to remember that he was my baby—no matter where he went.

The gate agent told me that I could not carry it because it was too big to put overhead. Then, she changed her mind when I told her why I wanted to bring it. They made room for me to take it home in the plane's first-class section.

Two exciting things happened at the airport before I boarded the plane.

First, I felt Omar's presence while standing in line waiting to speak to the gate agent. I read later that this was not rare. Feeling the deceased is like the "phantom limb" syndrome some report after losing a limb.[10] I've never lost a limb, but I felt my hair being ruffled by someone tall while I was in line. I turned around and didn't see anyone. It then dawned on me that what I felt was identical to what Omar used to do. From the time he was a child, he would run his hands through the back of my hair and play with it. After that, I had to go to the restroom to compose myself.

Second, I saw an angel. It happened as I was waiting for the plane to depart. We were more than two hours late leaving Atlanta, and Joel went to the counter to ask about the problem. While he was gone, a young man in his early twenties sat down and talked with me. He asked me what brought me to Atlanta and where I was going. I told him. He then comforted me by telling me that Omar was alive and that I would always have a relationship with him. I would just have to redefine the relationship: see him in signs and symbols such as dreams, the sunset, sunrise, butterflies, other people. After he said that, he was gone. I know God sent an angel to visit me, and I will hold on to that assurance until I get to heaven.

Omar's Articles Arrive

Omar's articles arrived within a week of our visit to Georgia, and Joel and I put them in the garage. I couldn't go through them. A few weeks later, I packed up the new suits I had purchased for him for Christmas and sent them to my brother, Anthony. I cried the entire time.

I was able to go through the remaining clothes Omar had at home within a few months of his passing. Fourteen years passed before I was able to go through the boxes. I kept his graduation gown, a few shirts, jackets, saxophone, Bible, and a few other items but gave most of them to the Star of Hope.

Dreams and Nightmares

"Which is the true nightmare, the horrific dream that you have in your sleep or the dissatisfied reality that awaits you when you awake?"

— *Justin Alcala*

Dr. David Jeremiah wrote:

> *Sunrise is inspirational and motivational. Sunrise says, yesterday the dark day is over, and a bright new day is on the horizon. Sunset brings closure to the day and hope for the morrow; sunrise brings great expectations and new possibilities. In fact, many people would love to bask in the beauty and flow of sunrise all day if they could.[11]*

*B*efore Omar's death, I was one of those people who loved the sunrise. It was different after he died. I often dreaded getting out of bed in the morning and facing a new day, for my days were often filled with death wishes and thoughts of suicide. I wanted to be with Omar!

I did everything I could to avoid thinking about his death. I stopped watching any show that had anything to do with violence because all I could see was Omar's body on the floor of that theater. I even found it difficult to listen to the news reports about someone murdered. And I shuddered when I drove on I-45 and had to pass the intersection of the theater.

Nevertheless, I couldn't avoid thinking about Omar after going to sleep. I didn't know if I would have a pleasant dream or a nightmare.

Dreams

Those who study dreams and nightmares tell us that they are how our subconscious mind copes with life and trauma. We work through our grief and feelings in our sleep. If you've experienced an intense loss, that may be the case with you. Some people remember their dreams, and others do not. Many people believe dreams are the deceased making contact.[12] That is not my belief, but I am so glad for my dreams about Omar. I don't remember all my dreams, and some are fragmented, but I can instantly recall several.

I had my first dream the day Omar died. It consisted of three scenes.

The first scene was of saints welcoming Omar into heaven. They were standing in a lengthy line on both sides, and Omar walked down the aisle between them. He had on a white robe and a bewildered look on his face. He didn't look like he was 22; he looked as though he was 14 years old.

The second scene was a vision of Jesus walking in the meadows of heaven with the palms of His hands opened and a welcome look on His face.

Then I saw an expansive room full of smoke. I don't know what that represented, but Bishop Ware felt it represented the presence of God as Isaiah described Him in Isaiah 6:1.

I reported this dream to Bishop Jerry Burley, my bonus brother, and his response surprised me. He told me that he had prayed for

God to give me peace and assurance that Omar was in heaven. God answered his prayer.

I had other reassuring dreams.

One of the most memorable was when I saw Omar in heaven all dressed up and standing against a vast white pillar with a big smile on his face. Another dream was of Omar and me walking through heaven. We were communicating, but our mouths were not moving. Our communication was through reading each other's thoughts. When we came to an immense golden gate, Omar told me that he had to go and would see me soon, but I couldn't go any further.

I thank God for these dreams. However, they were not recurring like the nightmares that haunted me.

Nightmares

I had recurring nightmares about Omar's death for several months—and I wasn't taking over-the-counter medication or prescription drugs that some doctors say may be the cause. In each nightmare, I was rocking my dead baby in my arms and rubbing his head. My tears formed pools of water that continued to pile up.

In the first nightmare, I was on the floor holding Omar's head and crying. My nightmares progressed until I dreamed that I was sitting in a bathtub holding Omar's head. The water from my tears was almost up to my neck and turned red from his blood. I read somewhere that we often have extraordinarily little information about sudden death, and troublesome dreams are where we work things through. If we wake from an unpleasant dream, our subconscious mind prompts us to do so. Some people believe you can "reprogram" your dream to have a different ending that is more comfortable. I couldn't.

Shortly after the "bathtub" nightmare, the Holy Spirit let me know that I was drowning in my tears due to a spirit of heaviness, and if I didn't give my cares to God, grief would consume me. So

I cried out to God and asked for His help. That was the last time I had a nightmare about Omar. Although, enjoyably, I've had many pleasant dreams about him over the years.

Returning to Work

"Do not judge the bereaved mother. She comes in many forms. She is breathing, but she is dying. She may look young, but inside she has become ancient. She smiles, but her heart sobs. She walks, she talks, she cooks, she cleans, she works, but she is not all at once. She is here, but part of her is elsewhere for eternity."

—Unknown

Out of Hibernation

On January 14, 1997, I returned to work one month after Omar died. I didn't have a smile on my lips before tears in my eyes, but I had to come out of hibernation. I also didn't want to go back too soon to compromise my effectiveness and efficiency, and I didn't want anyone to feel sorry for me. I just wanted them to empathize with me and give me space to heal.

My first-rate coworkers at Exxon gave me what I needed. Everyone went into the "help Sena heal her broken spirit" mode. My manager, Bill Dermott, was a compassionate listener and comforter. Until later, I didn't find out that he had someone from Human Resources (HR) talk to the department about interacting with me. Coworkers from other departments also offered me constant consolation and support.

Redefining My Life

One of the most challenging things about returning to work was redefining my life. Before Omar's death, I was the proud mother of two sons, and I spoke to my coworkers about Jay and Omar all the time, bragging about their achievements. After I got the news no one ever wants to hear, I became the mother no one ever wants to be. So how would I talk about Omar now?

I didn't want any of my coworkers to see my vulnerability. So when they asked me how I was doing, I soothed them with, "I'm fine." Of course, that was not true, for I was anything but "fine." I thought that was what they wanted to hear. My coworkers were sincere, but I didn't know if they were comfortable with any other answer.

Strength to Concentrate

Afterward, I found it hard to find enough strength to concentrate on work. Grief monopolized my every thought. As a result, I would frequently go into my office, close the door, and cry. In contrast, I was determined to demonstrate my faith in God before my coworkers. So I behaved like a person coming through the valley and on the way to victory.

Nominated by Coworker

Below is an excerpt of a letter my coworker, Dan Gibbs, wrote, nominating me for inclusion among the Outstanding Women in Houston in the Exodus Magazine. (they featured me in the August/ September 1999 edition). I included Dan's letter in this chapter because it had to be God who allowed me to demonstrate joy, strength, and composure in front of my coworkers after Omar died. I could have never done it on my own:

I knew something was wrong that December day in 1996 when Dr. Sena Thompson did not arrive at the airport for our planned business trip to Austin. Always the professional, Sena was the manager of our Regulatory Compliance Group at Exxon. Not only had I worked with and for Sena for several years, but I was blessed to have developed a close friendship with her based on our shared faith in God.

My worst fears were confirmed that December day when I learned that Sena's son, Omar, had just been murdered. I knew how much Sena loved her son and how devastating this tragic news must have been for her to hear and to bear. What followed was an incredible outpouring of love and support by so many friends who had obviously been touched by her life of love and concern for others.

But what was perhaps even more incredible was the strength, the composure, and yes, even the joy that she still expressed, along with her deep feelings of pain. Her answer to those who asked, "how can you hold up like this?" was simple: her deep faith in God. The Bible says that "the joy of the Lord is your strength." And the Lord was surely Sena's strength as it is now.[13]

Mom's Place

"I have not heard your voice in years, but my heart has conversations with you every day."

—Jessica Andrews

Dr. Charles Stanley wrote in the outline for his sermon, *The Believer's War Room*:

What are we to do with our trials, heartaches, and burdens? He (Jesus) says to go into an inner room, close the door, and pray to our Father in heaven. All of us need to learn how to talk to the Lord in private about whatever concerns us.

And sometimes that inner room becomes our war room as we fight our battles with sin, conflicts, decisions, and difficulties until we fully surrender in obedience to our God.

It's a private place. *God wants to meet with each of us privately so we can develop an intimate relationship with Him.*

It's a holy place. *When we habitually meet with the Lord in the same place each day, it becomes holy because it is set apart for worship and communion with Him.*

It's where our battles are fought. *... We need His guidance, assistance, and wisdom to know how to respond and what to do. There will be times when no one else can help us, but He is always there to comfort, strengthen, and encourage us.*

It is where we get instruction for the day. *We never know what awaits us each day, but God does. If we'll start the day in a quiet place, surrendering ourselves to Him and asking for direction and strength for whatever lies ahead, He'll walk with us through the day as our companion, guide, and protector.*

It is where we develop an intimate relationship with the Lord. *...It's only in our private times with the Lord that we come to know Him intimately and have the freedom to honestly and openly share our hearts with Him.*

It's where we weep over our trials and heartaches. *When we go into our prayer room and cry out to God, He understands and mends our broken hearts.*

It's where we are strengthened. *In this holy place we have the privilege of discussing every area of our lives. As we pour out our hurts, sorrows, and burdens, the Lord comes to strengthen us.*[14]

My Name for This Room

I call this inner room and war room Mom's Place. And before I close this section, I want to tell you about it. Everyone needs it after the death of their child and other atrocious losses.

Mom's Place was a gift from Omar. When he was in the first grade, his class went to a museum. I had given Omar a few dollars to spend, and he spent most of it purchasing a gift for me—a plastic sign that read, "Mom's Place," with directional arrows pointing to the left and right.

Before Omar's death, Mom's Place was my place to relax and kick back. I put the sign on my bedroom door to remind Jay and Omar that the bedroom was off-limits without knocking. After Omar's death, I was in a fathomless dark void, wondering whether I would ever resurface into the real world again. So, to help deal with my grief, I relocated Mom's Place to Omar's former bedroom, although I kept the sign on my bedroom door.

It was no longer a place of relaxation. Instead, Mom's Place became a place of request, remembrance, and reflection. That quiet place where I felt most safe and most terrified at the same time. I would retreat to Omar's bedroom to cry out in anguish or ask God for strength to get through the strain and agony.

Was Not a Utopia

Please understand me. Mom's Place wasn't a utopia. It was also a place of remorse, regret, and resignation. As I wrote about in the chapter *Everest of Indifference*, sometimes I left burdened with unanswered questions.

Mom's Place also couldn't stop me from thinking about Omar all the time. It was head-spinning. I could hardly think about anything for more than five minutes before my thoughts turned to Omar's death.

I would sit in the kitchen for hours pleading and begging God to bring Omar back. Even though he was deceased, God was a miracle worker and could have Omar walk through the door at any time.

I would go into the bathroom and kneel over the hamper, pleading and crying out to God to restore my baby's life. I cried so much that the top of the hamper became mildewed. Then, I would frequently leave my home alone to drive around and talk to God about bringing Omar back to life.

I wrote in *Returning to Work* that I would retreat into my office and cry out to God. The hurt was so intense I could hardly breathe. Sometimes I didn't think I could survive. I would walk during my lunch break through an underground tunnel and talk to God about bringing Omar back to life.

I would talk to Him about my suffering during my commute home, while I cooked dinner, and when I prepared for bed.

I Thank God for Mom's Place

Though it wasn't a utopia, I thank God for Mom's Place! I needed it then, and I need it now. No other place can provide the comfort and communion with God that Mom's Place offers. I pray you, too, will find a Mom's Place to commune with God.

ENTERING THE CRIMINAL JUSTICE SYSTEM

Photos No Mother Wants to See

"Before you tell a grieving parent to be grateful for the children they have, think about which one of yours you could live without."

—Lisa Bartsch Lahr

Closure Doesn't End with the Funeral

hen a child is murdered, the beginning of closure doesn't end with the funeral. First, you must deal with the criminal justice system. The purpose of the criminal justice system is to prosecute the offenders to the fullest extent of the law. Many murders of children remain unsolved, and the perpetrators never come to justice. This lack of justice places an indescribably heavy burden on their parents. Unlike these families, Omar's offenders were caught and tried for his murder. Because of this, there were lengthy legal proceedings before the trial.

My entrance into the criminal justice process started with looking at photos no mother wants to see.

No Mother Wants to See These

If you know me personally, it may not surprise you that my entrance into the criminal justice process started with photos. I love to take pictures of everything. All who know me well know that. I have boatloads of them, and I don't mind showing my amateur photography. If you visited our home, I could bring out albums, CDs, and DVDs of events.

My favorite photos are the ones I took of my children, Jay and Omar. I proudly display many of them throughout our home. But there are photos no mother wants to show. I'm referring to photos of the crime scene and those the Medical Examiner (ME) takes before performing the autopsy on your child's body.

Visiting the District Attorney's Office

January 22, 1997, Joel and I went to Assistant District Attorney Vic Wisner's (Vic) office. He was one of the prosecutors assigned to Omar's case. Vic had a large stack of photos, some of the crime scene and some taken before the autopsy. Joel, a former Police Chief, looked at all of them and thought it best if I didn't see any of them. Vic agreed. There was no way that I wouldn't see photos of my child! I asked them to take out the crime scene photos, and I insisted on seeing the rest, much to their dismay.

I Wasn't Prepared

I thought I had prepared myself for anything I saw—I hadn't. I can't begin to express to you how I felt when I saw Omar's lifeless body lying face down naked on the table with four gunshot wounds to the back. It's too hard to convey. At the time of this writing, it's been 25 years since his death, but I'll never forget it. The shock and horror of seeing his once healthy body riddled with bullets are beyond my ability to communicate. I thought my heart would stop beating!

Vic and Joel looked at me with concern as I viewed the photos. I told myself I wouldn't scream and holler, so I asked God for strength, and He held me together. I also felt some of God's pain and thought about how scared Omar must have been, running with his killer in pursuit, shots flashing.

After I finished looking at them, I went to the restroom for a good cry and a "daughter to father" talk with God. I couldn't understand it, and I didn't know why God allowed it. But I trusted God and believed Omar's killer would receive justice for what he had done.

Never Discussed Again

Joel and I drove home, and we never discussed the photos again. But, of course, we didn't have to; those wretched images are etched in my memory.

How Much Does an Organ Weigh?

"I will never forget the moment your heart stopped and mine kept beating."

—Angela Miller

Autopsy Report

*N*one of the documents I read concerning Omar's murder was as gut-wrenching as the Autopsy Report. An autopsy is a medical examination of a body to determine the cause of death.

I received Omar's Autopsy Report the same day I received the Investigator's Report—January 24, 1997. The report contained three sections: Blood and Urine Analysis, Pathological Diagnosis, and Postmortem Examination.

Blood and Urine Analysis

Dr. Ashraf Mozayani, Chief Toxicologist, Houston, Texas, performed the Blood and Urine Analysis to check Omar's blood for four substances, including ethanol and methanol. In addition, he tested Omar's urine for 11 substances, including marihuana, cocaine, opiates, methadone. Dr. Mozayani concluded that there were no traces of any drugs in Omar's system.

That was not surprising to me. Omar lived a clean life, and his body was well-conditioned. So I knew his tox screen would be clean, and there would be no drugs in his system.

Pathological Diagnosis:

Dr. Mozayani also performed the pathological diagnosis. His diagnosis was that there were four gunshot wounds of the back on Omar's body—three were through and through. Therefore, it was his opinion that Omar came to his death because of one gunshot wound of the back, homicide.

I had already read the Investigator's Report and knew the circumstances of Omar's death, so the diagnosis was not new to me.

The Postmortem Examination:

I thought I was ready to read the postmortem examination report as I had already read the other two accounts, and I had seen the pre-autopsy photos, but I wasn't. It was grueling. So I read the report with excruciating sorrow—as I am doing now, even as I author this book.

The report included a history of Omar's death (time, date, cause) and external and internal examinations of his body. Dr. Vladimir M. Parungao, Assistant Medical Examiner, Houston, Texas, performed the inspection.

External Appearance

The external appearance was how the body looked from the outside. Dr. Parungao wrote: "The body was that of a 22-year-old, black male who appeared the stated age. The body measured 72 inches in length and weighed 176 pounds. The body was well developed and well-nourished in appearance. The ears and nose were unremarkable. The mouth showed natural teeth. There was a short mustache and beard." The external examination also described the location of blunt lacerations and contusions on Omar's body (Omar fell on his face after being shot) and where the four bullets entered and exited his body. Dr. Parungao also indicated that Omar's "upper extremities showed no needle marks, no needle tracks, or any deformity."

Internal Examination

I read the external examination without throwing up, but I wanted to regurgitate when I read about the internal analysis of Omar's body. It described the gunshot wound track, how many millimeters of liquid and clotted blood were in Omar's body, injuries, and how much each of his organs weighed. That's what made me sick.

The report showed that every one of Omar's organs was unremarkable, meaning there was no disease. I expected that. He wanted to donate his organs. But the sheer thought of someone taking out my child's organs and weighing them was unbearable. What mother wants to know what her child's organs weigh? I didn't, but I do, and if your stomach is strong enough to read this part of my book, you know what Omar's organs weigh too. For instance:

Heart: The heart weighed 750 grams.
Lungs: The lungs together weighed 750 grams.
Liver: The liver weighed 1100 grams.
Spleen: The spleen weighed 100 grams.
Kidneys: The kidneys together weighed 250 grams.

As I read the report, I asked myself, "Did they put everything back in place or just throw his insides together?" I don't know and will never know. All I know is that *it made me sick to my stomach! It still does!*

Pretrial Proceedings

"The weird, weird thing about devastating loss is that life actually goes on. When you're faced with a tragedy, a loss so huge that you have no idea how you can live through it, somehow, the world keeps turning, the seconds keep ticking."

—James Patterson

Several proceedings were finalized before the trial began:

Arraignment

An arraignment is a pre-trial court hearing to charge a person with a crime formally. Omar's perpetrators, Brian Gonzales (Brian) and his accomplice Jason Garcia (Jason), were arrested on December 11th and arraigned before Judge Lloyd Douglas Shaver on December 13th. They were both held without bond.

Pretrial Conference

February 11, 1997, Joel and I went to Harris County Courthouse for a brief pretrial conference held in Judge Shaver's courtroom. The conference's purpose was to allow the prosecutors and defense attorneys to meet with the judge to work out the details of Brian's trial, review evidence and witnesses, and set a time-table for the trial. In addition to those affiliated with the court, two other people were present, sitting as far as they could from where Joel and I were sitting.

During the conference, Vic explained the process to us and talked to us about life vs. death. I showed him a photo of Omar that I took in New Orleans on an alligator tour and asked him if we could bring in character witnesses for Omar. He said probably not, but that he would put Joel and me on the stand to testify.

First View of Brian Gonzales

My first view of Brian Gonzales was when the sheriff brought him into the courtroom in shackles. He was about 5'5", weighed about 140 pounds, and was wearing an orange prison jumpsuit. I was enraged when I saw him. I hated him. I saw him as a thug, crook, and pathological sociopath. The word "hate" is not too firm because that is how I felt about Brian. I *hated* him! *How could he cold-bloodedly shoot Omar four times in the back?*

Brian had pleaded guilty but was asking for leniency. His attor-neys, Joe Bailey and Bob Sussman motioned to suppress evidence about his prior criminal acts so the jury couldn't use it in deliber-ating their verdict. Judge Shaver denied their request and said the evidence was admissible.

Before we left, Vic told Joel and me that the two persons in the courtroom were Brian Gonzales' parents. He said the father is self-employed, and the mother works for an oil company. I hoped it wasn't Exxon, where I was employed. They looked like law-abiding citizens. *What went wrong?* I want to scream at them; *why did you let your son kill my baby?!*

Vic said the case would go to trial late summer or early fall if there was no plea bargaining. I didn't want to hear anything about plea bargaining. It had to be death!

Jury Selection

The jury selection process for Brian's trial started on September 19, 1997. In the pool of potential jurors were three black females and one black male. Judge Shaver asked if anyone could not serve due to health or religious beliefs or had difficulty being objective. A few stood up, and Judge Shaver dismissed them. Then, the prosecutors struck all the blacks that remained.

The jury ended up being composed of three Hispanic males, three white males, and six white females—one who was eight months pregnant, as well as two alternates. I was upset at first when Vic cut the black potential jurors since Omar was black. I also felt it was a defense strategy to put an eight-month pregnant woman on a capital murder jury, but I knew the outcome was in God's hands. I was certain Brian would get the death penalty; it didn't matter about the jury composition.

After warning them not to read any case coverage, Judge Shaver dismissed the jurors and told them to be back in the jury box at 10:00 a.m. Monday, September 29, 1997, for opening arguments.

Let's Make a Deal

"From the outside looking in you can never understand and from the inside looking out you can never explain."

—Compassionate Friends

*I*n the interim between the pre-trial conference and jury selection, I received a call from the prosecutor (Vic) asking if I would accept a plea bargain and letters from Brian's attorneys and mother.

Letter to Prosecutor

On March 11, 1997, I responded in writing to Vic.

My response:

"As I mentioned to you on the phone a week or so ago, I believe there is no proper punishment for Mr. Gonzales other than death. He took Omar's life in a premeditated, cold-blooded fashion, and I strongly believe his life should also be taken.

I beg you to consider Omar's life when determining whether to accept a plea bargain or life for Brian Gonzales. In 40 years, Omar would have been only 62 years old—a relatively young man by most standards. Gonzales will be 59. He'll still have a lot of his life before him, and he would have had the benefit of waking up every morning to a new day for 40 years, while he denied my son that benefit by pumping four bullets into his back.

Life in prison is not the proper punishment for Mr. Gonzales. Death is the only proper punishment. Mr. Gonzales played God when he took my son's life, and his life should also be taken. When he killed my son, he knew the consequences but pulled the trigger again and again and again and again. If he is allowed to die, it will be much more humane than the way he maliciously ended my son's life.

Thank you again for the opportunity to give my input."

Letter from Brian's Mother and Attorneys

Brian's attorneys and mother still tried to persuade me to change my mind.

June 12, 1997, I received an envelope from John B, Holmes, District Attorney, containing a letter from Brian's mother. July 29, 1997, I received a letter from Brian's attorneys appealing to my sense of mercy.

I was not interested in plea bargaining; I wanted Brian to die! I didn't have an ounce of pity for him. He was an evil animal and had snatched Omar from our family and friends and me as Omar was beginning to sprout his wings and fly. Though I was a Christian minister, I wanted to retaliate. So I plotted his death in the fantasies of my mind: I would slowly torture him then shoot him 20 times in the back as his mother watched him suffer.

He had also negatively affected my attitude toward Hispanic males. Whenever I saw a young Hispanic man, it made me think of Brian. It didn't matter that I had Hispanic friends.

What's more, I had settled my viewpoint on capital punishment. If the forensics are independently corroborated and aligned with the evidence, I have no problem with pre-meditated murderers being put down.

I didn't respond to Brian's mother, but I responded to Brian's attorneys on August 12, 1997:

"While I understand your position as Brian's attorneys and Brian's mother's position, let me state unequivocally, unabashedly, and unbending that I believe Brian should receive the death penalty for Omar's murder. It has nothing to do with mercy or forgiveness or justice; it has to do with punishment for what Brian did to my son.

You also commented in your letter, 'to show our good faith, we also want to pass on to you an idea of preserving the memory of your son.' While that comment is admirable, if my son had not been murdered by your client there would be no need to preserve his memory. However, you can rest assured that Omar's memory will forever be in my heart and in the hearts of those who knew him. My son was an outstanding person who spent his life doing nothing but helping others and trying to make this world a better place. Moreover, he was a wonderful son to me; and was one of my best friends. Not a day goes by when I don't think of Omar and how terribly I miss him. His death has decimated our entire family.

Furthermore, you asked for a meeting to discuss these matters. I believe a meeting would be an unproductive use of everyone's time; therefore, I respectfully decline."

Asking for the Death Penalty

I was so pleased when Vic informed me a couple of weeks after I replied to Brian's attorneys' letter that the state would ask for the death penalty for Brian. He said the evidence was quite clear. Brian had pleaded guilty to Omar's death, and it was a solid capital murder case. *Thank You, Father. I hope he gets what he deserves!*

THE TRIALS

Scales
of Injustice

"I never sympathize with the accused unless there's a chance the accused is not guilty, but I certainly don't ever sympathize with the criminal."

—*Clint Eastwood*

The Scales

*W*e want scales to be fair, balanced, and accurate. Only when they're balanced can something be equal. Dishonest scales give one preference over another. The reality is, there are outside factors that can change the weight. So, whose scales do we use to bring justice? God's scales, of course! Psalm 37:28 says, "For the Lord loves justice and does not forsake His godly ones."

The Charges

The Capital Murder trial of The State of Texas vs. Brian Gilbert Gonzales began September 29, 1997, at the Harris County Courthouse, 301 San Jacinto, 5th Floor, in Judge Shaver's courtroom. Capital Murder is the most severe crime in the state of Texas.

It is the state's only offense punishable by death. The state charges persons with capital murder if they intentionally kill someone while committing or attempting to commit certain crimes. For example, in Omar's case, robbery. The penalty for capital murder is life in prison without parole (40 years) or death.

Brian was 19 years old when he killed Omar and 20 when his case went to trial. The State accused him of robbing the theater where Omar worked and knowingly and intentionally murdering Omar. The trial outcome came down to one question: Will the jury believe that Brian knowingly and intentionally killed Omar, or was Omar's death unintentional and accidental? The Prosecution's case was that Brian did intend to kill Omar. The Defense's case was that Brian didn't intend to kill him.

The Duration

It took seven days to move the wheels of injustice. The trial lasted three days, and the punishment phase lasted four days. There was a total of 23 witnesses—12 during the evidence phase and 11 during the punishment phase.

I was drained physically, mentally, and emotionally by the time the trial began. I had also gotten comfortable with pain; but not with bleeding, as Clinical Psychologist Dr. Amanda Spencer described it. Even though it was tough, I had come to accept God's will.

I'm grateful that I had a good support group. My sisters Bert and Elyse, and late brother-in-law, Tez, flew in from Philadelphia and stayed with Joel and me until the trial ended. Several of my friends attended every day.

I rejoiced that judgment had finally come Brian's way. The trial was also a perfect time for God to display His trustworthiness and act on my behalf. I did not doubt that God would be merciful to me by executing Brian for killing Omar.

I took journals with me every day of the trial. Judge Shaver and the prosecutors didn't object to my taking notes. I tried to capture everything exactly as it occurred. Even now, I can feel every emotion I wrote about and my heartbreak from the trial's outcome. Please find a seat in the courtroom as I summarize what happened. It will give you more insight into why I titled my book "When You Think God Isn't Fair."

Monday, September 29, 1997

The morning of the trial, Elyse, Bert, Tez, Joel, and I prayed together before leaving the house. On the way to court, we heard a report about the trial on the radio. It was wrong. The information was Omar was murdered during a robbery because he refused to turn over the money. *Can you get it right, please?*

When we arrived at the courtroom, Brian's parents were outside the door. His father extended his hand, and I shook it, even though I didn't want to. Regardless, I realized he didn't kill Omar—his son did. Reporters were also there and followed the trial. Elyse's heart was palpitating; mine was calm. *God has this!*

When we entered the courtroom, the prosecutors, Vic Wisner (Vic) and Kelly Siegler (Kelly) explained what to expect. There would be three days of trial. We would have Thursday off, and the punishment phase would start Friday. I was so grateful that Vic and Kelly were the prosecutors. They were both known for their successful prosecutions. Kelly had never been unsuccessful in prosecuting a death penalty case. *Thank You, Father!*

My Second View of Brian Gonzales

Brian looked different the second time I saw him. He was dressed up and sitting with his attorneys, Joe Bailey and Bob Sussman. To me, it was like dressing up a snake. He was still a cold-blooded killer, and I hated him for what he had done to Omar.

Opening Statements

The trial started at 11:00 a.m. with an opening statement from the prosecutors. Vic briefly told their account of Omar's murder and summarized the case they intended to present to the jury. They had plenty of ammunition in their arsenal to prove Brian's guilt and made the death sentence likely.

Brian's attorney, Bob Sussman, gave an opening statement for the defense after the prosecutors finished their account. It was like watching a side-show intended to cause the jury to be distracted from the real issue—Brian Gonzales was a heartless murderer! Mr. Sussman tried to portray him as a human being rather than a vicious animal. He couldn't paint Brian as a victim, so he painted him as an upright young man from a good family who had gone astray. Mr. Sussman also admitted that the defense looked for something from a cross-section of Omar's life to misalign his character, such as searching through school records, talking with our neighbors, but couldn't find anything.

Prosecution Evidence

After the opening statements, the prosecutors built a case against Brian. Vic and Kelly alternated in presenting their evidence. I thank God that they were not controversial prosecutors who faced recall for their progressive pro-criminal policies. Instead, they were an advocate for Omar. They were persistent in their prosecution and fought long and hard for the jury to make a capital murder verdict with a death penalty sentence.

I listened intently as the specifics of the crime were discussed in detail.

Witnesses

The prosecution called six witnesses the first day. All of their testimony pointed to Brian's guilt.

The first witness called was the police officer who arrived at the scene after Omar's murder. He testified that he arrived at the murder scene on December 10, 1996, at 2:48 a.m. When they arrested Brian the following day, Brian told him that he shot four times at Omar, and all four bullets ricocheted and hit him in the back. Kelly asked him how likely it was that it happened that way. He said, "very unlikely."

The second witness was the 911 operator who took the call about Omar's murder. Kelly played the 911 call before the operator testified. On the call, the manager was hysterical and begged them to come. She called three times before the police arrived.

After lunch, the security guard who patrolled the complex where the AMC theater was located testified. He said that he saw Omar running with Brian in chase. He also heard the shots. Brian was five to six feet behind Omar when he shot him.

The fourth witness called for the prosecution was the manager of the AMC theater where Omar worked. She testified that she and Omar were closing for the night. Omar went to the back to turn off the light switch. As soon as he turned it off, the manager noticed someone in the theater. She screamed and ran out. She didn't warn Omar; she just ran. She said she heard four shots but didn't look back.

Enactment of Omar's Murder

After the AMC manager testified, Kelly and Vic enacted what happened. Omar ran from the theater with Brian chasing him. I didn't have to play the horrible events of Omar's death in my head; minute by minute, they were graphically replaying it in the courtroom. Kelly said the bullets seemed to be fired in rapid succession, and Omar saw the flames in that dark room when he was hit.

I don't have words to describe how I felt when they enacted the shooting. It was beyond distressing to see the way Brian brought down Omar's body. The gun that killed Omar was so large—it was an enormous .45 caliber! I felt the need to scream at them to put that horrid gun away!

When Bert whispered, "He was running for his life," it made the sting worse. I just wanted to elope from the courtroom as fast as I could and throw up. I thought about Omar running away from Brian and him running after Omar. *Did he have time to think about his fate, or did it happen so quickly that he didn't have time to think? Did he think he was going to die? Did he think of me? How long did he suffer before he died?*

A Needed Break

There was a short break after the prosecutors enacted Omar's murder. I had to get myself together, so I went into the restroom. Guess who was there? You're probably right: it was Brian's mother! She told me how sorry she was about Omar's death. I didn't want to hear it. I told her directly that I was praying that her son would get the death penalty for murdering Omar. She told me she understood, but she was a Christian and prayed to God for mercy.

I didn't say anything then; but I think that was my first hunch that the trial wouldn't go as I hoped. I felt a little like Jonah. God sent him to Nineveh to tell the people that He would destroy them for their terrible deeds. Jonah hated the Ninevites and ran the other way. He changed his mind after spending three days in the belly of a massive fish. The Ninevites repented, and God didn't destroy them. Jonah became angry with God and told God that he knew God would change His mind if they repented because God is merciful, compassionate, slow to get angry, and filled with unfailing love (Jonah 4:1-2).

Last Witnesses of the Day

The last witnesses of the day were two of Brian's friends, Terrence Brooks and Marcus Emory. Terrence testified that he and Brian were the ones who purchased the gun that killed Omar. Marcus testified that Brian came to his home right after the shooting, saying that he had "messed up," things had gone wrong, and he had shot someone, maybe one time. Marcus said Brian was remorseful. He also said that Brian had discussed the "killing zone" with him. Brian knew about guns because he and his family were hunters.

Court Adjourns

The court adjourned around 5:00 p.m. The testimony hurt us all. Kelly and Vic apologized to us about how the prosecutors presented the evidence but told us everything had to be perfect to get a guilty conviction.

Tuesday, September 30, 1997

More Witnesses

The prosecution's evidence and witnesses continued. They called five people to testify: a police officer, the Medical Examiner (ME), a firearms expert, and two detectives: Detective Ortiz and Detective Davis. Their evidence also pointed to Brian's guilt, so I started feeling better about Brian receiving the death penalty for killing Omar.

The police officer testified about taking the bullet the ME extracted from Omar's body to the crime lab. It matched the gun that Brian and Terrence had purchased.

The ME testified that Omar died from four gunshot wounds to the back. Of the four shots, one was fatal. He showed where Omar was shot and how the bullet traveled. He said all were more than two feet away, accounting for no powder burns on Omar's body. The ME said there was no way to determine which bullet was first, which shot was last. He also said he had no way of telling how far Omar would have been able to run.

The firearms weapon expert testified that Omar was killed by a .45 caliber gun and about the size of the bullet. He said it was a big gun that could put a big hole in a person's body. He also said it came from the same weapon that Brian had purchased.

Detective Davis testified that he arrived at the theater and found Omar on the ground and deceased with apparent gunshot wounds to his body. He spoke to the manager of the theater, who told him what had happened. Detective Davis further stated that he identified Omar from a valid Texas driver's license on his body. He then testified that he found one vehicle parked in the theater's rear when he went to the theater. It was a 1987 black Chevrolet Cavalier convertible. He later spoke to Terrence Brooks, who told him that the car belonged to Jason. Brian told Terrence that he and Jason attempted to leave the scene of the murder but could not get the vehicle started and had to leave the car in the rear of the business.

Detective Ortiz was the detective who took Brian's confession. He read the confession in full. Brian stated that he needed money to help his father because his father was depressed. He owed the IRS about $10,000, and Brian wasn't making enough. Brian said he knew a way to make "quick money." Additionally, Brian confessed that he shot at Omar and continued to shoot because he was scared. He didn't know he had hit him and didn't know Omar was dead until the next day when he heard it on the news.

Grief on Hold

I had put my grief on hold throughout the trial other than crying when the prosecutors enacted Omar's death. It is only by the grace of God that I did not need professional psychotherapy or have post-traumatic stress disorder (PTSD) when the ME testified. The Holy Spirit kept me from yelling and being removed from the courtroom. Instead, I just closed my eyes and pleaded with God for a guilty verdict.

Somehow, I felt better after Detective Davis finished testifying. After that, all I could say to myself is *Look at God!* What are the chances that someone commits a murder and their vehicle doesn't start? It had to be divine intervention! So I was more confident than ever that Brian was going to get the death penalty. *Thank You, Father!*

Character Witness for Omar

I was a character witness for Omar and the last witness called before the prosecution rested its case (Joel didn't testify). It wasn't hard to be a character witness for Omar. There was no victim-bashing campaign that so many parents or concerned friends who have lost loved ones have to endure throughout the trial.

Vic had already presented evidence about Omar's exemplary life. Along with that, I had so much more to say about Omar. I welcomed the opportunity to tell others about my wonderful son.

I never imagined that I would be so nervous. I was shaking so much that I could hardly walk to the witness chair. Every eye of the jurors was on me, and the judge's eyes seemed so penetrating. I numbly answered Vic's questions to keep from breaking down. When he questioned me about Omar, he concentrated on what a fantastic young man Omar was, all the positive feedback he had received from persons who knew Omar, and his academic achievements. He then asked me how Omar was as a son, and I told him some of the things I've written about in the chapter, *A Glimpse of "The Prince."*

I was able to keep my composure until Vic asked me how I found out about Omar's death and when was the last time I saw him alive. Then he spent a lot of time talking about Omar's death's impact on Jay and how I dealt with Jay since Omar's death. The last question Vic asked was, "How did you feel about burying your son?" I can't remember everything I said, but I did write in my journal that I said, *"No mother wants to bury her son. When I buried Omar, I buried a part of my future."*

I was relieved when I left the stand; but I was honored to say something on Omar's behalf.

Defense Cross-Examination

Throughout the trial, Brian's attorney, Joe Bailey, had crossed examined each of the prosecution's witnesses to create doubt about their credibility; but I felt he was unsuccessful. It was apparent that Brian knew what he was doing when he killed Omar. Mr. Bailey didn't have any questions for me. He was kind and took my hand as I left the stand. It felt strange.

Defense Evidence and Witnesses

After the prosecutors rested their case, it was time for Brian's attorneys to present their defense. They didn't call any witnesses. Brian didn't testify.

Wednesday, October 1, 1997

The events of the day included closing arguments and jury deliberation.

Closing Arguments

Closing arguments started at 9:30 a.m. Vic presented the case for capital murder vs. felony murder (felony murder means the murder was accidental, not intentional). He stressed to the jury that Brian knowingly and intentionally murdered Omar to keep Omar from identifying him as the person who robbed the theater. Vic also told the jury that Brian belonged to a gang and was linked to a previous crime.

Kelly ended the argument by telling the jury that they should close the courtroom if they acquitted Brian of capital murder. It was hard to hear her presentation. She repeated several times how Brian executed Omar—shot him in the back four times. She also said Brian had no reason for killing Omar other than that Omar saw his face and could identify him, so he had to kill him.

Brian's attorney, Bob Sussman, then gave his closing argument. He started his comments with the remark I made about no mother wanting to bury her son. He admitted that Omar's death was a horrible murder but tried to prove beyond a reasonable doubt that Brian didn't kill Omar knowingly or intentionally. Mr. Sussman did an excellent job for a defense attorney, but I wasn't moved by what he said. What Brian did was indefensible. I hoped the defense didn't move the jury.

Prosecution Rebuttal

In a criminal trial, prosecutors wield a giant sword because they have the last comments. Kelly's blade was razor-sharp. She did everything right and ripped Mr. Sussman's closing argument to shreds, proving again beyond a reasonable doubt that Brian intentionally and mercilessly murdered Omar. She even demonstrated the impossibility that Omar's death was an accident and urged the jury to ignore what Mr. Sussman said.

When Kelly finished, she and Vic both appeared confident that the jury would return a guilty verdict. I was satisfied too. To me, it wasn't a complicated case. It was evidence and the word of 11 witnesses (excluding my testimony). All the pieces of the puzzle added up—Brian deserved death for murdering Omar.

Elyse asked me if I was pleased with the proceedings. I told her I was upset by the defense attorneys' attempt to make Brian appear remorseful and say he acted without malice. But I trusted God to give Omar justice.

Jury Deliberation

When Kelly and Mr. Sussman finished their closing arguments, Judge Shaver informed the jury of the appropriate law and what they must do to reach a verdict. The jury retired to deliberate about 10:20 a.m. I hoped they understood what was at stake with their ruling. I noticed that a couple of the jurors seemed tired or bored during the trial. Joel said one of them fell asleep—I didn't see him nod, but his eyes were closed. *Wake up! He killed my baby!*

It was agonizing waiting for the jury to deliberate. Every minute seemed like an hour. We expected it to be a short deliberation. Anyways, the evidence was so damaging I didn't think the jury would have a challenging time convicting Brian.

The jury had not returned by noon. Bert said there was no doubt in her mind that Brian would be found guilty, but her heart was pounding. Elyse and I wanted to knock on the door and ask what was taking so long. I asked Kelly if she was concerned. She said no. She would be worried if they came back with a verdict after 5:00 p.m.

The Verdict

God came through for me! At 2:00 p.m., Judge Shaver announced that the jury had reached a verdict: "Guilty of the crime of first-degree murder." When he read the verdict, it took everything I had to control myself. We couldn't show emotion because the judge had admonished everyone not to do so. But my family, friends, and I were ecstatic. After the jury went out, we hugged Vic, Kelly, and each other. Brian's family was distraught. It didn't bother me one bit. I couldn't imagine how they could have anticipated a favorable outcome for this soon-to-be-dead monster.

I called my job and informed them of the outcome. Everyone was glad for us. I also spoke to the reporters covering the trial about giving thanks to God for what He had done. The evening news covered the story.

Our family prayed that night and thanked God again before going to sleep. I was so glad that the jury would do justice for Omar.

Thursday, October 2, 1997

There were no court proceedings. My family and I went to the AMC theater where Omar died to piece things together.

PUNISHMENT PHASE

Friday, October 3, 1997

The punishment phase began to decide Brian's sentence: death or life in prison. Three witnesses were called.

Silvio Rodriguez

The prosecutors called one witness: Silvio Rodriguez, manager of another AMC theater Brian had robbed. Mr. Silvio testified about how he was robbed at gunpoint and kidnapped by Brian and his accomplice. When they told him to take a ride, he lost it. It was hard to hear his testimony, especially when Vic asked him what was going through his mind. He said he thought his life was ending, and he thought about his mother. I felt that was going through Omar's mind too, and I felt a lot of tension as he testified.

After Mr. Silvio's testimony, Joe Bailey, Brian's defense attorney, called two witnesses to convince the jury that Brian was not deserving of death: a psychologist specializing in Texas Department of Correction inmates and Gilbert Gonzales, Brian's father.

The psychologist testified that Brian had psychological disorders that may account for his behavior. But, considering what he had just said, the prosecution ripped his testimony apart.

Mr. Gonzales testified that Brian killed Omar because of him. He owed IRS, had his electricity turned off several times, and had marital problems. He also said that Brian was a good kid who was an underachiever, didn't know what he was doing, and shouldn't die. Although Mr. Gonzales appeared sorrowful, his testimony didn't faze me—it seemed staged.

Court Adjourns

The court adjourned around 5:00 p.m. until Monday, October 6, 1997. My family and I talked about the day's events and prayed together before going to bed. I couldn't sleep, waiting for Monday to seal Brian's fate.

Monday, October 6, 1997

When my family and I arrived in the courtroom, Vic spoke to us and said everything seemed to be going well; keep on keeping on. He felt that the jury was favoring death, but of course, that was speculation.

Several witnesses testified:

Brian Gonzales

The first witness was Brian Gonzales. When he testified, I had an opportunity to hear Omar's killer's voice for the first time, and it was chilling! I could hardly stand to look at him. I couldn't roll my eyes at him or give him an ugly look, but I wanted to.

Brian testified that he robbed the theater because his parents needed money, and he felt financially responsible for his family. He said Omar saw his face and started running. He said he didn't run after Omar; he just shot him. My heart was pounding so much that I thought it was going to jump out of my chest. Joel was upset beyond measure. *How could Brian believe it was okay to kill Omar just because his parents were having financial trouble?*

Brian's attorney, Joe Bailey, questioned him about his remorse and told him to tell our family how he felt. Brian said he was remorseful and apologized to Omar and me for killing Omar. He also said he hoped I could forgive him one day. Not!! I didn't believe one word that he said, and I despised his testimony. He attempted to put reasonable doubt in the mind of the jurors. If one juror fell for his lies, he couldn't receive the death penalty. To me, Brian's testimony was not credible. He was very theatrical, and he had no remorse. He deserved death!

Brian's family cried as he talked. I also cried a little when Brian testified, not for Brian, for my baby! I was fuming!

Break

We took a half-hour break before Brian continued his testimony. During the break, Kelly asked me why I was crying when Brian spoke. I told her it hurt so much to know that Omar saw his killer's face. She asked me not to cry when Brian's mother testified because the jury may think I sympathized with the family.

Brian's Testimony Continues

After the break, Vic poked holes in everything Brian said and caught him in numerous lies, mainly why he killed Omar. Brian testified that he would not have attempted the robbery had there been a police presence in the theater or perhaps in the parking lot. He said he knew there was no surveillance video to capture the shooting or security guard inside the theater.

Then Brian changed his story. He said he didn't want to kill Omar but killed him out of loyalty to his gang, and he didn't want to look like a sell-out. Vic said, "That's not what you told the police. You told them you killed Omar to help your family." He asked Brian why he had a loaded gun if he didn't intend to kill Omar. Brian said he didn't know. Vic questioned him about the safety on the gun. Was it on when he entered the theater? Brian said no. Vic said, "You didn't want to shoot yourself, did you?"

Next, Vic asked Brian again why he killed Omar. Brian said he got scared. Vic said, "Yes because Omar saw you and could identify you." Vic then said to Brian, "You probably got ticked because Omar ran, and you couldn't do to Omar as you had done to Silvio Rodriguez—torture him and threaten to kill him."

Before he finished questioning Brian, Vic had him reenact how he killed Omar. I couldn't stand to see it again! As Brian showed how he shot Omar, I whispered a prayer to God, thanking Him for sparing Omar from being tortured. There was no doubt in my mind that Brian would have done the same thing to Omar as he did to Mr. Rodriguez and then kill him.

Brian's Character Witnesses

After lunch, several persons testified on Brian's behalf. I didn't journal the testimony of most of them, but I did write about the testimony of Brian's mother, Mrs. Gonzales.

Brian's Mother

The defense saved their prime character witness for last—Brian's mother. She was probably Brian's last hope. Vic and Kelly asked great questions to pull answers from the defense witnesses, but they didn't cross-examine Brian's mother. I understood this because the defense attorneys didn't cross-examine me.

Mrs. Gonzales pleaded for Brian's life. She said Brian made a terrible mistake; but he was a good kid who tried to help his family. The jurors didn't seem to be paying too much attention to her, and I was glad. I thought her testimony was likely to impact the jury significantly. I could empathize with Mrs. Gonzales but knew I would vote for the death penalty if I were a jury member—and I would feel good about it! Yes, I heard that death is more compassionate than spending the rest of your life in prison. I didn't think so; I wanted Brian to die!

The defense and prosecution rested after Mrs. Gonzales pleaded for Brian's life.

Closing Arguments

Kelly asked for the death penalty again. She described Brian as looking like a choir boy, acting as though he had a hardship. But, she said it was just a front. Brian was a 19-year-old gang member, and his shooting of Omar was a direct hit! Kelly also talked about my grief, emphasizing the impact of Omar's death on our family, especially on Jay.

Brian's defense attorneys asked the jurors to spare Brian's life.

Tuesday, October 7, 1997

Jury Deliberations

Judge Shaver charged the jury, and the jury retired to deliberate about 11:40 a.m.

As the jury deliberated Brian's punishment, I thought about how smoothly the trial had gone. I understood why Vic and Kelly were known for their prosecutorial skills. They were superb, almost textbook perfect, and worked together like clockwork. Everything was on schedule. They made eloquent closing arguments. I knew we were well on the way to seeing Brian getting his just deserts—a death sentence.

"Hung" Jury

The jury deliberated until 9:15 p.m. and had not reached a decision. I didn't expect it to be that long. Vic informed us that it took so long because seven of the jurors, including the eight-month pregnant juror, wanted to give Brian the death penalty, and five wanted him to receive life in prison. The long deliberation was too much for the pregnant juror. She became hysterical until she became sick, so they had to stop deliberating. Someone called an ambulance for her.

My heart started palpitating uncontrollably. I looked at Kelly, and I knew this wasn't good. Then I asked her what would happen if the pregnant juror went into labor. Kelly said they would wait until the baby was born and have her come back to court. Kelly also said she didn't know what the juror's doctor would say. If the stress of the trial was harmful to the baby, they might have to declare a mistrial. In that case, Brian would automatically get a life sentence. She also said that the judge might accept a verdict from fewer than 12 jurors.

I could see the disappointed look on Vic and Kelly's faces when the juror got sick. Yet, despite everything, Vic appeared to be optimistic. He said he couldn't be sure, but he expected the jury to return with the death penalty. Possibly they may not have a verdict until the next day, so "be calm." I shook his hand and hugged Kelly to thank them for everything they did for Omar and our family. I'm sure Kelly saw my tears.

My family and I were at a loss for words and didn't talk too much that night. It was late, and we had to return to court the next day at 8:30 a.m. I had mixed feelings about the trial. Brian was guilty and deserved to die. There was no mitigating evidence, and I thought he was a future threat. But, on the other hand, I didn't know if the state would be willing to try him again.

I also knew Brian's fate was in God's hands. I continued to pray for strength, grateful that the jurors convicted Brian of capital murder but disappointed that the pregnant juror was upset with the sentencing deliberation. But, come what may, I knew that God was in control. He knew how everything was going to end.

Wednesday, October 8, 1997

We arrived at court about 8:15 a.m. Judge Shaver had to wait until the pregnant juror returned from her doctor's appointment before starting court. Vic seemed concerned.

Brian's Trial is Over

Brian Gonzales' trial was over at 4:00 p.m. The defense strategy paid off by selecting the pregnant juror. The bailiff gave judge Shaver a note from her doctor asking to excuse her from the jury. Vic and Kelly were both crying. They knew they had a conviction for the death penalty. But, of course, they couldn't force her to stay. I cried too. It was as though a ton of bricks had fallen on me.

Vic started to blame himself for not getting the death penalty. He said he or Kelly should have taken the pregnant juror to her doctor instead of letting her go without them. At a minimum, Judge Shaver should force her to return to court and tell him why she couldn't continue to deliberate. But who would be responsible if something happened to her baby? Of course, hindsight is 20/20.

Plea Bargain

Instead of declaring a mistrial, the prosecutors offered the defense team a plea bargain: a mandatory life sentence of 40 years, with no parole. And Brian had to plead guilty to the robbery and kidnapping of Mr. Rodriguez, which carried a 60-year sentence. For that, he had to serve 30 years before being eligible for parole. The sentences run consecutively; so, Brian would be in jail for a total of 70 years. He would be 90 years old when he left prison.

The other alternative was to hold another trial and risk the chance of Brian being found not guilty of capital murder or being found guilty and given the death penalty. If there were another trial, it would probably take another 18 months before it could begin. I told Vic that I didn't want to go through another ordeal.

After the trial, Joe Bailey complimented my family and me for how we conducted ourselves. He then asked for a hug, and I hugged him. I even hugged Brian's mother and told the news media who covered the trial that I accepted God's will.

God isn't Fair!

I couldn't sync my heart with my lips. I was a power-keg of emotions when I got into the elevator. The last thing I wanted to do was accept God's will. I was upset with Him! He allowed Brian to escape death, and I felt betrayed by His unfairness. I know some would consider a life sentence a slow death. 2066 was the earliest date Brian could get out of prison, he would be eating prison food the rest of his life, and I'd be in heaven for a long time by then. That didn't matter to me. I was upset! I thought about the entire ordeal that I had gone through following Omar's murder. I could have avoided a demanding trial and didn't have to waste my time if I knew the prosecutors would accept a plea bargain. *It wasn't fair!*

Postscript:

Attorney Murray Newman posted an article on April 8, 2008, about the outcome of this trial:

> *Harris County prosecutors Vic Wisner and Kelly Siegler were trying the one death penalty case that they didn't get the death penalty on.*
>
> *The defendant's name was Brian Gonzales. He had shot and killed a young man named Omar Jamal Aycox while robbing an AMC movie theater. Mr. Aycox had graduated from college that year and was working at AMC before going to the University of Texas to study for a graduate degree in International Business. Mr. Aycox also had a mentally disabled older brother that he had a special bond. His brother thought that the sun and moon were set by his baby brother.*
>
> *Vic Wisner and Kelly Siegler tried the case through the guilt/innocence phase as if Omar Aycox was their own child. They told the jury that Omar was shot four times in the back as he fled from Mr. Gonzales during a robbery.*
>
> *They proceeded into the punishment phase with the same passion, asking for the death penalty. There was no doubt that Brian was guilty. In fact, his lawyer admitted that he was and asked the jury for mercy. As I sat in the courtroom, I felt no compassion for Brian for killing Omar, and I hoped beyond hope that he would receive death for what he had done. But he received mercy. The only thing that saved Brian Gonzales from death row was a pregnant juror that went into early labor during punishment deliberations, thus resulting in a mistrial.*[15]

Note: The pregnant juror did not go into early labor.

Repeat Performance

"I will always miss my child. Never ask me if I'm over it, even a little."

—*Unknown*

*B*rian's trial was over, and I was disappointed in God, but our time in court wasn't over. We had to attend the Capital Murder trial of Brian's accomplice, Jason Thomas Garcia.

Jason's trial began Monday, November 10, 1997, in Judge Shaver's courtroom. He was just 16 years old at the time of Omar's murder and 17 when the trial started. The State charged him with capital murder because under Texas law, when someone is killed during certain crimes, everyone committing that crime is held responsible—even though they didn't pull the trigger, have a gun, or intend to kill. Jason was certified as an adult after a psychological evaluation.

Pre-Trial Proceedings

Before Jason's trial, there were two pre-trial proceedings: jury selection and a Suppression of the Evidence hearing. Judge Shaver and the prosecutors allowed me to take notes during the pre-trial proceedings and the trial. A summary of my journal notes is below:

Jury Selection

The jury was selected Thursday, November 6, 1997. I didn't record the jury's composition.

Suppression of the Evidence Hearing (SOE)

Judge Shaver held the SOE on Friday, November 7, 1997. Joel and I attended the hearing and sat next to Jason's father. Jason's mother wasn't there. His father hung his head. I guess he was so ashamed of what his son had done.

When I saw Jason for the first time, he had shackles on his feet and hands. I was surprised by his appearance. He looked like he was 14, weighed about 125 pounds, and was about 5'1" or 5'2". Jason also looked scared. That didn't concern me. He helped Brian kill Omar!

During the SOE, Jason's defense attorney asked Judge Shaver to throw out Jason's written and oral statements given to the police. He wanted Jason's oral statement thrown out because he said the officers did not read Jason his rights before he made his statement. He wanted the written statement thrown out because Jason had an IQ of 90 and didn't understand when the magistrate talked to him.

Detectives' Testimony

At the beginning of the hearing, the detective who interrogated Jason testified that he had confessed to being an accomplice in Omar's murder. I had obtained a copy of Jason's written statement (Juvenile's Statement) from the courthouse clerk long before the SOE hearing because it is a public record, so I was familiar with what he had written. Therefore, I could understand why his lawyers wanted to suppress it.

Jason's Written Statement

Jason's written statement was entirely different than Brian Gonzales' testimony. It was a lengthy statement, so I'll just recap a portion of it here:

"...Brian and I got to the theater about 10:20 p.m., and we bought tickets to see Set It Off. We went and watched the movie. At the end of the movie we went over to another movie theater room that was empty. We could see the manager's office, the concession booth, and the front doors from the empty theater room. I didn't know where the manager's office was but Brian said that he did. Brian cocked his gun, a Ruger .45, and we waited for everybody to leave. The plan was that we would wait for the manager to walk by the door and to pull the gun out on him and ask him how many people were left in the theater. Then to call anyone that was left down there and have the manager take him to his office and find out who was the head manager. They were then going to get the head manager to open the safe.

...We waited in the empty theater room and then all of a sudden all the lights went out and it was pitch dark. One of the theater doors was open and the other was closed. Brian saw the manager walk by the door and he went out. Brian pointed the gun at the manager and told him to 'freeze.' The manager froze for a second and then I heard a lady scream, then Brian looked over to the lady that was screaming and that is when the man manager took off running across the lobby towards the box office. The lady who was screaming took off out the front doors and that is when I came out of the room.

Brian took off running after the man manager and then Brian stopped and shot at the man manager twice, then after the second shot he slowed down, taking his time and aimed, he shot three more times. I took off running towards where Brian was, before he fired the last shot I hit his hand down towards the ground. I grabbed Brian and pushed him to the side.

...I want to say that I am sorry to have been a part of the guy getting killed. I was stupid for going along with Brian and I want to apologize to the family of the guy who died. It wasn't supposed to happen like this and no one was to have gotten hurt. I have thought about what happened and wish that I could have done something to prevent this from ever happening. I know that what I did was wrong, and that I will be punished in some way. I don't want Brian to get away with what he did. I know that it has bothered me a lot but Brian hasn't seemed bothered by it at all."

Motion to Suppress Denied!

I prayed that God would allow the prosecutors to enter Jason's testimony into evidence at his trial. Praise God! Judge Shaver denied Jason's attorney's SOE motion, and Jason was on his way to trial for Omar's vicious murder!

Monday, November 10, 1997

Jason's trial began. Several media attended, but they did not report it as much as Brian's trial.

The Prosecutors

For Jason's trial, the prosecutors were the same ones who prosecuted Brian Gonzales—Vic Wisner and Kelly Siegler. They told me that the trial wouldn't be "as hard as Brian's" because the prosecution was not seeking the death penalty.

Jason Enters the Courtroom

Jason entered the courtroom about 11:00 a.m. He was neatly dressed in casual attire and looked like a frightened little boy. I was sure the jury was going to take that into account.

Plea Bargain

The jury didn't have to take anything into account. True to what Vic and Kelly said, the trial wasn't as long as Brian's. It lasted one day. There were no witnesses.

Before the trial started, Judge Shaver asked Jason if he would accept the plea bargain that the state was offering him—45 years for aggravated robbery instead of a 40-year life sentence for capital murder without parole. He would have to serve 22-1/2 years before he could be eligible for parole. Jason's lawyers wanted him to accept the plea bargaining, but Jason insisted on going to trial.

Jason's Trial is Over

Jason's lawyers took him to the judge's chambers a few minutes later. They told us that Jason had accepted the plea bargain when they came out.

After court, Joel and I gave Jason's father our card and told him to tell Jason if he ever wanted us to visit him, we would. He said he had lost a child at six months of age, and he understood our pain. He was crying and kept saying he was sorry. He also said he was a Christian and had talked with his pastor, who said perhaps God allowed this to happen to save his son from the road he was on. Mr. Garcia also told Jason that he owed his life to Omar and had to make something of it. If not, Omar died in vain.

Different Emotions

I had no anger and hatred for Jason when I left the courtroom. Instead, I pitied him for destroying his life. He had no previous detention history; he had just gotten in with a bad seed—Brian Gonzales. I also was not upset at God. I felt He had been fair. I was also glad to move on with my life and get Jason and Brian's trials behind me.

DISCONNECTING FROM GOD

Faith Struggle

"Trust me; I know how it feels.

I know exactly how it feels to cry in the shower so no one can hear you, and watching for everyone to fall asleep so you can fall apart, For everything to hurt so bad you just want it all to end. I know exactly how it feels."

—*Anonymous*

My Determination to Move On

My determination to move on after Jason's trial should have been the end of my story. Now I had more time to put the finishing touches on a Praise & Prayer Explosion I was coordinating to honor God and those involved in ensuring Brian and Jason received the penalties they deserved.

It wasn't. Brian's sentence weighed heavily on my heart, and I struggled with faith in God's justice. As I recounted earlier, I didn't have an issue with Jason's sentence because I thought he was just a misguided child.

I Believed the Bible

My faith struggle wasn't because I didn't believe the Bible. On the contrary, I knew God's Word was true and contained no errors—if God said it, that settles it. And, although I didn't under-stand why He allowed Omar to die, I stood on every word of Deuteronomy 32:3-4 (NLT): "I will proclaim the name of the Lord; how glorious is our God! He is the Rock; his deeds are perfect. Everything He does is just and fair. He is a faithful God who does no wrong; how just and upright he is!" I also knew that God engi-neers some adversities, such as the man born blind described in John 9. Furthermore, I knew He gave Paul a thorn in His side to keep him from being prideful (1 Corinthians 12).

But Brian's sentence was in a class by itself. I couldn't rationalize the contradictions I was experiencing based on reality and what I knew about God's character. Brian deserved to die. God's cruel injustice challenged my core assumptions about Him and turned some of my most fundamental beliefs upside down. If God is just, why does He allow injustice to touch the lives of those He loves?

How Can I Trust God?

Similarly, since I couldn't trust God to bring about justice fol-lowing Omar's death, how could I trust Him in other areas of my life? And what about all the Scriptures in the Bible about pun-ishment for the shedding of man's blood such as Genesis 9:6, "Whoever sheds man's blood, by man's blood shall be shed. For in the image of God He made man," or Deuteronomy 19:6, "Thus you shall not show pity: life for life, eye for an eye, tooth for tooth, hand for hand, foot for foot"?

While I was struggling, I certainly could identify with what the father said in Mark 9:24, "I believe, help my unbelief." I was able to conceal my faith struggle, acting as though everything was okay and keeping my thoughts between God and me. It took a lot of emotional energy, but who does a Christian minister confide in when she's struggling with her faith in God?

Everest of Indifference

*"It's enough to drive a man crazy; it'll break a man's faith.
It's enough to make him wonder if he's ever been sane.
When he's bleating for comfort from thy staff and thy rod
And the heaven's only answer is the silence of God."*

—Andrew Peterson

K. W. Osbeck writes, "Often into our lives come discouragements and heartaches that we cannot understand. As children of God, however, we must learn never to question the ways of our sovereign God."[16]

Sliding Down a Slippery Slope

I never learned the lesson about never questioning God. Instead, I believe we can ask God honest questions, and I asked God to explain His actions about Brian's sentencing. I realize that Brian's sentence may seem like a small matter to you, and I concede that my reaction appears overblown as I'm authoring this book. But it was monumental to me 25 years ago.

I didn't know I was sliding down a slippery slope leading to what Ken Gire calls the "Everest of Indifference" when I asked God to explain His actions. According to Mr. Gire, climbing Mt. Everest is a metaphor for our pursuit of God to find answers to our most searching questions. An "Everest of indifference" is when God remains silent. He writes:

> *Unanswered questions can form an impasse in our relationship with God that is Himalayan in its expanse. Stopped there, we look to the highest mountain in that range, to the God we once knew—or thought we knew—and the God whose paternal arms we once felt wrapped so protectively around us now seems an 'Everest of indifference.'*
>
> *With that sudden sting of awareness comes a blizzard of questions.*
>
> *Amid the blizzard, as we stand there in the shivering cold, we sometimes lose our bearing and we wonder.*
>
> *Did we ever feel the arms of a heavenly Father around us? Or was it just a break in the weather and a patch of sudden sun upon our skin?*
>
> *Were the answers we once heard the sound of his voice? Or was it simply the sound of our own voices echoing off the cliffs?*
>
> *Was he always like this, and the wispy clouds of our spiritual imagination merely obscured the reality? Or did he somehow change?*
>
> *And did we do something to cause that change?*
>
> *Or was it something we failed to do?*[17]

Tapped Into My Feelings

Mr. Gire is concise in describing God's response to my questions. The only answer I received was His deafening silence. This cold-shoulders treatment stunned me, amplified my torment, and shook the ground under my feet. I never had a problem that God and I could not discuss. When He didn't give me point-by-point answers as I expected, I felt as though I was climbing Mt. Everest without my climbing gear.

Mt. Everest is not a playground. It is located in Asia and is Earth's highest mountain above sea level—29,032 feet tall. It's difficult to breathe on Mt. Everest because oxygen is only 34% of its concentration on the ground below.[18] Unfortunately, many people die climbing, with one death for every ten successful climbs. A sobering statistic for anyone who reaches the summit is that you have a 1 in 20 chance of not making it down again.[19] Many who reach the top come back with physical and psychological problems from the climb.[20]

I tried to encourage myself by reading and meditating on the book of Job. God allowed him to suffer severely without telling Him why. Job asked many questions for a long time before God spoke to him. And when God responded, He didn't answer Job's questions. Instead, He asked Job many questions that Job couldn't answer (chapters 38-41). So Job went to his grave not knowing why God allowed him to suffer so harshly.

No Comfort

Reading about Job didn't give me the comfort I was seeking, and God's silence had changed me. How could He say I'm His daughter, whom He profoundly loves but let me twinge with pain?

And while I knew in my head that God would somehow, someday turn all this around for good in my life, the intensity of the distress made me start to doubt God's care for me. I felt that His timing was questionable, His lack of intervention was hurtful, and His promises were situational. Left alone with those feelings, I couldn't help but feel disappointed that God wasn't doing what I assumed a good God should do.

Faith Failure

"Just because my eyes don't tear doesn't mean my heart doesn't cry. And just because I come off strong, doesn't mean there's nothing wrong."

—*Anonymous*

Emotional Disconnect

*Y*es, I titled this chapter correctly, and it is hard for me to write it because I am truly ashamed of my anger and frustration at God for not answering my questions. Still, I promised you I would be transparently honest and authentic.

Simply put, I disconnected emotionally from God. When we connect to Him emotionally, we learn to value and love the things God values and loves. I didn't. His continued silence was the tipping point. I loved God, but my faith in Him had crumbled because He violated our intimacy. As a result, I still couldn't trust Him without reservation and remained suspicious of what He would allow to happen to me in the future.

Moving Away Wasn't Blatant

My moving away from God wasn't blatant; it was subtle. It was like a hairline fracture. A hairline fracture is a small crack or severe bruise within a bone. Not allowing yourself time to heal between activities is often a factor in getting this injury. The most common symptom is pain. Other symptoms include swelling, tenderness, and bruising. Ignoring the pain caused by a hairline fracture can result in the bone breaking completely.[21] I was already broken.

Moving away from God didn't take long either. It all happened within a month after Jason's trial. I tried to look on the bright side and concentrate on how far God had brought me since Omar's death. And He had. But when my faith failed, trying to look on the bright side wasn't enough to sustain me. I could identify with the writer of Psalm 73:1-2 (NLT) when he wrote, "Truly God is good to Israel, to those whose hearts are pure. But as for me, I almost lost my footing. My feet were slipping, and I was almost gone."

Covered Up My Hurt

I covered up my hurt with "silent spirituality." I went to church and acted as though everything was well with God and me. I wrote encouraging notes to my coworkers and friends. I prayed with those who were going through tough times. I even continued working on the Praise & Prayer Explosion scheduled for January 24, 1998, to thank God for His goodness to me. Yet, I knew that my relationship with God wasn't what it used to be or should be.

Is this a shocking confession? Unfortunately, it is to most people, and it should be!

RECONNECTING
WITH GOD

Trust Transfer

*A*ccording to "The Grief Recovery Handbook":

> *Loss of trust events are experienced by almost everyone and can have a major, lifelong, negative impact. Is loss of trust a grief issue? The answer is yes. And the problem of dealing with the grief it causes remains the same. Grief is normal and natural, but we have been ill-prepared to deal with it. Grief is about a broken heart, not a broken brain. All efforts to heal the heart with the head fail because the head is the wrong tool for the job. It's like trying to paint with a hammer—it only makes a mess.*[22]

I can say a resounding "Amen!" to the authors' writing. My grief over Omar's death and Brian's sentencing demanded a lot of my attention and energy. I knew I didn't want these two life-changing events to destroy me. But, if I wanted to have peace, comfort, and hope, I had to reconnect with God: (1) I missed my intimacy with Him; (2) the void I had in my heart from being detached from Him was too obvious to ignore; (3) my faith had always been my comfort when everything else seemed bleak and hopeless; (4) "it is in God that we live, move, and have our being" (Acts 17:28).

As Sheila Walsh writes, "I had to decide: Do I believe God's Word or not? Do I believe God is in control? Do I trust God? ...The bottom line was this: Do I actually believe what I've said for years, or do I believe only when life makes sense?"[23]

I believed.

Miriam and Stuart Bundy tell us that the demonstration of our faith is trust:

> *Do I believe He is who He says He is? And, if I do, the demonstration of my faith is trust.*
> *If I believe He is sovereign, then I trust Him, even though I have no control and no certainty of healing.*
> *If I believe He is love, then I trust Him, though I sometimes feel isolated and alone.*
> *If I believe He is faithful, then I trust Him, though I cannot see what is happening.*
> *If I believe He is just, then I trust Him, though I did not bring this on myself.*
> *If I believe He is righteous, then I trust Him, though everything seems all wrong.*
> *I believe that God is sovereign.*[24]

Reestablishing My Faith

To reconnect with God, I had to re-establish my faith in Him and make a trust transfer. Likewise, if you are disconnected emotionally from God, you'll have to do the same, for that is where you will find strength and hope to go on—even after the death of your child.

I define a trust transfer as relying on God entirely instead of relying on our strength, knowledge, perception, or reasoning

(Proverbs 3:5). The Bible also stresses that God is faithful (1 Corinthians 1: 9) and utterly dependable. Numbers 23:19 (NLT) says, "God is not a man, so he does not lie. He is not human, so he does not change his mind." Hebrews 13:8 says, "Jesus Christ is the same yesterday, today, and forever."

We don't just say "I trust God" because it is the Christian thing to say. And we don't just sing words of trusting God because it's in the praise song. James Airraz writes:

Trusting God means putting full confidence in Him. It is undivided. Nothing is left behind. It does not require pre-conditions because when we trust Him, we begin to realize that it isn't about what we feel but about what He's doing. It's not about what we understand but about who He is. ...It means trusting Him through highs and lows when it doesn't make sense.[25]

Trusting God also means believing that He is working things that aren't good out for your good (Romans 8:28) and believing that His silence does not mean that He is indifferent.

My path back to the intimacy I shared with God wasn't easy, and it wasn't short. My faith in God failed because of the misconceptions I had about Him. I didn't know Him personally as well as I thought I did. I was looking from a distance at what God did or didn't do. Since I was looking at God from a distance, I didn't understand His ways. Because I didn't understand His ways, I couldn't trust Him.

Therefore, to make the trust transfer, I needed my perception of God's sovereignty, love, and fairness revised and turned upside-down. To do that, I had to learn the truth about God's character, correct my misperceptions, and rely on His Word and promises. I discuss this in the next chapter.

Correcting Misperceptions

"Trying to figure out God is like trying to catch a fish in the Pacific Ocean with an inch of dental floss.

— Matt Chandler

*P*erception is a way of regarding, understanding, or interpreting something. A misperception is a mistaken belief or idea about it. As noted in the previous chapter, after Omar's death and Brian's sentence, I had misperceptions about God's sovereignty, love, and fairness that had to be corrected before I could reconnect with Him. Below are the crucial truths I learned about God's character that helped broaden my understanding of Him and transition from disconnect to reconnect.

God's Sovereignty

God's sovereignty is His wisdom, power, and righteousness all wrapped into one. That means He is the divine Ruler over all things, all people, all times. Psalm 24:1 tells us that "The earth is the Lord's and everything in it." God knows us intimately and has numbered our days before we were born (Psalm 139:16). 1 Timothy 6:15 (NLT) reminds us that He is the "blessed and only almighty God, the King of kings and Lord of lords." And like the lyrics to the song, *Sovereign*, as sung by Daryl Coley, says, "God can do whatever He wants to, when He wants to, and how He wants to because He's sovereign."

God's sovereignty also means that His purpose is always right and good even if it doesn't look that way from our perspective (Isaiah 55:8-11; Romans 8:28).

Could God have stopped Brian by changing his heart, diverting the trajectory of the bullet or jamming his gun? Absolutely! Could He have prevented the pregnant juror from getting sick? Of course! Does He sometimes supernaturally override the sinful intentions of those who would seek to harm others? Yes! Proverbs 16:33 (NLT) tells us, "We may throw the dice, but the Lord determines how they fall."

Although I cannot figure God out, I now trust His sovereignty and pray that you will too. I know this is difficult for those who have lost a child. And yet, there is no way to have peace without trusting God's sovereignty, even when we don't understand and are hurting. Only God knows why these things happen, and I will not "play God" by attempting to give a rational explanation. I also know that we live on promises, not on answers. As Apostle Paul said in 1 Corinthians 13:12, "For now we see in a mirror, dimly, but then face to face. Now I know in part, but then I shall know just as I also am known."

God's Love

1 John 4:16 tells us that "God is love." I had preached about God's love and taught about God's love, but I didn't factor God's love for Brian into the equation when He murdered Omar. I erred because I was comparing God's love to human love. That is a flawed means for determining God's love. Quite often, demonstrations of human love are fragile and failing. When the criterion for being loved goes away, so does the love.[26]

In contrast, God's love surpasses human comprehension. It is lavish, high-level, unconditional, sacrificial, unwavering, irreversible, and perfect. It knows no bounds. His love is not temperamental or based on what we do. He's always gracious, merciful, and kind. He cannot retract His love, despite our faults and craziness, or He would not be perfect love. He loves us in the good times and in the tough times, when we're obedient and when we're evil. It includes those who have murdered our children.

John 3:16 tells us that God loved us so much that He sent His only begotten Son [Jesus Christ] to the world that all who believe in Him will not perish but have eternal life. Romans 5:8 tells us that the greatest demonstration of God's love was when Jesus laid down His life for us while we were sinners. He hung, bled, and died on Calvary's cross so we could have access to God and the only way to heaven (John 14:6).

Because of His love for us, God promised to be with us, even when He is silent. Our responsibility is to linger in His presence long enough to get our minds quiet and our hearts open to hear from Him. Then, cast all our anxiety on Him because He cares for us (1 Peter 5:7).

For example, Isaiah 43:2 tells us that He will be with us when we pass through the waters. We have His Word in Matthew 28:20 that He will be with us always, even to the ends of the earth. He promised in Isaiah 49:15-16: *"Can a woman forget her nursing child, and not have compassion on the son of her womb? Surely, they may forget, yet I will not forget you. See, I have inscribed you on the palms of My hands; your walls are continually before Me."*

There's one more thing I'd like to talk about before I discuss God's fairness—God not only loves us, but He also wants us to love Him. Love requires free choice. So when God created His sinless world, He knew there was the possibility we would choose evil, although that wasn't His will.

Our first parents, Adam and Eve, chose evil. Genesis chapter three tells us after God created them, He placed them in a paradise called the Garden of Eden. God told them they could eat from all the trees in the garden except the tree of the knowledge of good and evil. Satan enticed them to eat from the forbidden tree. They sold humanity out when they chose to disobey God, and sin and its consequences entered the world.

Satan is still enticing people to sin. That is why there is so much suffering in the world—including the paralyzing anguish of losing a child. The Bible tells us when we encounter evil, "we are not fighting against flesh and blood enemies, but against evil rulers and authorities in the unseen world, against mighty powers in this dark world, and against evil spirits in the heavenly places" (Ephesians 6:12, NLT). So, when someone chooses evil over good, please don't blame their actions on God. Instead, let the knowledge of His love for you bring you comfort and peace.

God's Fairness

When people ask if God is fair, they often ask from a human perspective—meaning, does God deal with people in the way they deserve? As you have read throughout this book, this is the perspective I embraced. For me, fairness was equality—everyone receiving what they deserve—including Brian. As a result, I ended up expecting God to do what He didn't promise.

When I gained a clearer understanding of God, I found out, true to the title of my book; God isn't fair—from a human perspective.

God's Justice

From a biblical perspective, however, God is fair. His "fairness" is synonymous with "Just," which refers to justice. God's justice is an indispensable part of His character. So when we say God is "Just," it means He always does what is right, and He does it consistently, without partiality or prejudices.[27] (Deuteronomy 32:4; Psalm 111:7-8, Isaiah 61:8; Acts 10:34; Revelation 15:3; 16:7).

Therefore, we can't measure God's actions by the criminal justice system. The criminal justice system governs by facts, evidence, rules, and the pursuit of the truth. It is not perfect, although it should try to be perfect. But God is not trying to be perfect; God is already perfect and perfectly righteous in how He treats each of us.

Human Perspective of Fairness vs. God's Justice

Understanding the difference between a human perspective of fairness and God's justice helps us appreciate how loving and merciful God has been to us.

Let's think about a few things for a moment:

Have you ever stopped to think that our children belong to God? We came into this world naked and with nothing. We have children because of the grace and mercy of God. Is it fair that many people are infertile? No!

Or consider this. Many women can conceive, but their children don't enjoy one day of life on this planet. Many years ago, I used to travel to Chicago frequently. When I did, I always went to the Museum of Science to see the prenatal development of children who died in their mother's womb—especially the beautiful little blond-haired stillborn baby whose mother carried him for nine months. Each time I went, I wanted to cry out to him, "Please open your eyes, little one!" Some of you reading this book may know the grief of having a stillborn child. My heart goes out to you. Some of you are like me. You've had miscarriages. Mine was at four months; yours could have been sooner or later. Is that fair? No!

Here's another question: Have you ever walked through a cemetery and looked at the dates on the tombstones? For me, more than half of them died at a much younger age than I am. That may be true of you, too. But, whatever your age, there are millions who are younger than you or me who have died from accident, illness, or disease. Is that fair? No! Where is the God of equity?

The list goes on, but you get my point. The real question that I should have been asking God is not, "Why are You so unfair?" but "Do I want You to be fair to me?" No, I want God to be Just! The universe stands guilty before God (Romans 3:19). If God were fair, He would kill all of us. "For all have sinned; all fall short of God's glorious standard" (Romans 3:23). Good behavior, generous gifts, sacrificial acts, hours of prayer are not what exempted us. It was our Lord and Savior, Jesus Christ, the incomparable Son of God.

When we sinned, God's justice could not overlook it. But His justice was satisfied when He sent His own sinless Son, Jesus Christ, into the world to be our substitute. Jesus was perfect in every way, yet He was betrayed, arrested, mocked, punched in the face. He was stripped completely naked and beaten 39 times with a whip made of leather straps with sharp, rugged pieces of metal, wire, glass, and jagged fragments of bone. He carried a heavy cross, had spikes driven through his hands and feet, and then was hung on that cross for six hours in unbearable agony until He paid the penalty for our sins.

Is that fair? No! But "He became sin for us who knew no sin that we could become the righteousness of God in Him" (2 Corinthians 5:21). "Christ died for sins once for all, the just for the unjust, so that He might bring us to God" (1 Peter 3:18). And in the courtroom of heaven, even though we were guilty, and deserved the death penalty, God, the righteous Judge, extended mercy to us, declared us not guilty, and gave us life. "Who shall bring a charge against God's elect? It is God who justifies. Who is he who condemns? It is Christ who died, and furthermore is also risen, who is even at the right hand of God, who also makes intercession for us." (Romans 8:33-34).

Thank God for justice! If you are like me, you are praising God right now because He isn't fair! And, while we're at it, let's also give Him praise for His sovereignty and love!

Are You Kidding Me?

"You'll never know how strong your heart is until you forgive who broke it."

—Unknown

*C*orrecting my misperceptions about God drove me back to where I should have been all the time—into His tender, loving, and compassionate arms. It was a glorious feeling to have my intimacy with Him restored. I was now ready for the Praise & Prayer Explosion.

Forgiveness

The Explosion was spectacular! I discuss it in more detail in the chapter, *Blessings from Teardrops.* After the Explosion, I felt fully connected with God.

However, without being affected by my feelings, the Holy Spirit gave me a task to complete before I could truly make that claim. I'm talking about forgiveness. God had forgiven me, but I had not forgiven Brian and Jason. You see, His mercy extends even to the unlovable—Brian, Jason, and me. Psalm 103:3 tells us that He doesn't deal with us according to our sins or reward us according to our iniquities (Psalm 103:10).

It would be grand to say that I forgave Brian and Jason as soon as the Holy Spirit told me to, but that would be a bald-faced lie. It took a long time before I could forgive them from my heart. I knew it was the right thing to do because the Holy Spirit will never lead us in the wrong direction. Instead, when He impressed upon my heart to forgive the two men, I disobediently answered, *"No way, not today, not ever! I'm not going to do it; I'll just have to walk in rebellion!"*

To My Credit

To my credit, I had come a long way. Before Brian's and Jason's trials, "forgiveness" wasn't even in my vocabulary. Instead, I felt disgusted and intolerant. I kept mental records of what they had done and held them hostage in my mind so I could replay their offenses repeatedly. I would examine every little point of what happened. Their evil deed pierced my heart like a dagger that I couldn't completely pull out.

On top of that, even if I did forgive Jason, I didn't think Brian was redeemable. So I couldn't move on as though nothing had happened! I also agreed with Jason: Brian didn't seem to be bothered by Omar's death at all. So w*hy are you asking me to forgive them? They didn't ask me to forgive!* And yes, I am an ordained Christian minister.

No Condemnation

I'm grateful that the Holy Spirit didn't condemn me for hanging on to my bitter spirit and unforgiving attitude. He just continued to impress forgiveness on my heart lovingly. He led me to attend a Justice for All rally in Austin, TX. My local Parents of Murdered Children (POMC) chapter chartered a bus, and I rode to Austin with several chapter members. On the return trip to Houston, I sat next to one of the POMC leaders. He pointed out a young lady, named Stephanie, who a robber shot in the face and killed her roommate during a break-in at their home. She had forgiven her attacker. I made it a point to speak with her when the bus stopped.

The bus stopped at a restaurant, and I introduced myself to Stephanie and told her about my conversation. I let her know that I admired her faith, but I didn't think I could do it. Stephanie said that she felt the same way about her perpetrator but found out it was possible. The key was in knowing that we can only forgive someone for what they did to us. God gave life, and when Brian killed Omar, it was an act against God. However, I could forgive Brian and Jason for what they took from me.

Her words planted a seed within me. I tried to forgive them. But I couldn't do it when I thought about the future joys with Omar they had stolen from me.

Then the Holy Spirit started leading me to books on forgiveness. One book that stands out in my memory is a book by Liberty Savard, *Shattering Your Strongholds*. In that book was a prayer for forgiveness. I read that prayer over and over with my lips, but my heart wasn't in it.

Cruising Time

I needed a vacation to get away from hearing the Holy Spirit talk to me about forgiving Brian and Jason. So, like Jonah, I decided to take a cruise (well, Jonah didn't take a cruise). But, even on the voyage, the Holy Spirit continued to pull at my heartstrings. He reminded me of what Psalm 139 said: "Where can I go from Your Spirit? Or where can I flee from your presence? If I ascend into heaven, You are there, If I make my bed in hell, behold, You are there. If I take the wings of the morning And dwell in the uttermost parts of the sea, Even there Your hand shall lead me, And Your right hand shall hold me." (Psalm 139:7-10).

This time, I knew the Holy Spirit wasn't going to give me an out. So, I surrendered to Him and forgave Brian and Jason from my heart as I knelt and cried in the teeny-weeny bathroom of the Carnival Cruise ship. I realized if I trusted God, I had to obey Him—even when it was difficult.

Write Letters

Then came the nuclear bomb! Shortly after I returned home from my cruise, the Holy Spirit prompted me to write a letter to Brian and Jason informing them that I had forgiven them. Though I sincerely wanted to obey because I knew I couldn't have true fellowship with God without trusting and obeying Him, this was beyond forgiveness! I was dumbfounded and refused to do it, questioning Him about what He was asking me to do.

Are you kidding me? I can't do that! I know I'm a minister, but this is cruel and unusual punishment. I forgave them. That should be enough!

Things change. For those of you who are Christians, you know when the Holy Spirit speaks to your spirit, you will have no rest until you do what He says. His leading is often subtle, taking the form of an impression or nudging in your heart to do something. Alternatively, when you don't respond, His leading can be more dramatic, such as troubling your spirit every moment of every day to remind you of your disobedience. Well, I had many restless days and nights because I couldn't bring myself around to writing letters to Brian and Jason.

Shamefully, it took me almost three years after Omar's death before I could write to them. Here is what I wrote:

August 31, 1999

Dear Brian [and Jason]:

Greetings in the name of our Lord and Savior, Jesus Christ!

My name is Dr. Deborah Thompson. You and I have met, but we do not know each other. I'm Omar Aycox' mother—the young man you murdered December 10, 1996. You will probably be as shocked to receive this letter as I am to write it, but it is a letter that must be written, for God has put it on my heart to do so. In fact, He has laid it on my heart for a long time. I fought it for a long time, but I can't fight it anymore.

What I want to say to you, Brian [Jason] that I forgive you for murdering my son. I can't begin to tell you how Omar's death has affected my family and me. I still walk around with a big hole in my heart, and I am a living witness that someone can live with a broken and bleeding heart. I will love and miss my son until the day I die. All who knew Omar, including his father and mentally disabled brother, will love and miss him until they die also.

But also, I will always be pained by Omar's death. I realize that vengeance belongs to God, and forgiveness is my duty. For certainly, my prayer every night is that God will forgive me as I have forgiven my debtors. I forgave you over a year ago, for as a minister of God, I could not preach about the love of God without doing so, but I really didn't know if I could bring myself to write you to tell you that I had. Not that I wasn't sincere, but I didn't know how you would receive it.

Well, now you know, Brian [Jason], that God has laid on my heart to forgive you. I hope you receive it in the spirit by

117

which it is given. But I must tell you that God does require something of you. That is to live your life in such a way that you can bring glory to Him. Remember, you may be imprisoned, but a child of God is never bound. Use this opportunity to be a witness to all around that Jesus Christ is the way, the truth, and the life. Let your light so shine among all the persons you meet, so they can see your good works and glorify God.

If you aren't a Christian, my prayer is that you would get to know God in the pardoning of your sins as Omar did. I thank God that Omar was a fine young Christian man, and because of that, he has been given eternal life. And because he has been given eternal life, I have the assurance that I'll see him again one day. And my prayer is that you too have the assurance of eternal life, Brian [Jason]. If you don't, all you have to do is to confess your sins to God and ask Him to come into your heart. Read the book of Romans, especially Romans 10:9. Do what it says, and you will be saved. You see, even though God doesn't love sin, He loves sinners. For my Bible lets me know that we have all sinned and come short of the glory of God. And only God can give us the peace that we need to make it through life. In fact, He can give you perfect peace that passes all understanding (Isaiah 26:3). And the reason why we have peace is because we become new creatures when we give our lives to Christ (2ⁿᵈ Corinthians 5:17).

As I close, I want you to know that I will continue to lift you before the throne of God, Brian [Jason], for I know God is able to work things out for the good of those who love the Lord. Stay prayerful and continue to lift up your eyes to the hill—God is not through blessing you!

If you find it in your heart to do so, please write to me and let me know how you're doing. Also, please let me know if you would like me to send some books to you that will strengthen your walk with the Lord. Also, if you'd like to talk to me face to face, let me know that also.

Take care, Brian [Jason], and stay encouraged. Read the Psalms every night—especially Psalm 90 and Psalm 91. May the road rise to meet you, may the wind always be at your back, may the rain fall softly on your meadows, and may God hold you in the palm of His hand until we meet again.

Yours in Christ,

Elephant Lifted

I'm so glad the Holy Spirit was relentless in prompting me to forgive Brian and Jason and write to them. It lifted the elephant of bitterness from my heart.

I received a reply from Jason dated November 23, 1999. He told me how sorry he was for Omar's death, said he had accepted Christ as his Lord and Savior, and thanked me for showing him how we're supposed to love one another. He also asked me to write to him more about Christ to strengthen his relationship with Him.

I did write to him about Christ. He and I have corresponded several times over the years. He even sent me a copy of the testimony he gave when he gave his life to Christ. I also received a letter from his father asking for forgiveness, to which I gladly extended.

I have not heard from Brian, but I did meet the father of one of Brian's friends. He told me that his son stopped being friends with Brian after he murdered Omar. Brian wrote his son and told him he received a letter from Omar's mother extending forgiveness. As a result, Brian's friend was also willing to forgive him.

BETTER DAYS

Wounded, But Healed

"God will not look you over for medals, degrees, or diplomas but for scars."

—*Elbert Hubbard*

Thought for Today

Taped on the wall of our home office, next to Omar's photo, is a Thought for Today, which reads, "I will not let the disappointments of this world discourage me. What I see as an ending, God sees as a bright and glorious beginning" (Author Unknown). These words became my daily confession. I would read them every time I came into my office.

You've been reading my book, so you know that I didn't fully internalize these words after Omar's death. The wounds were too extensive. Sadly, some were self-inflicted. After I reconnected with God, I determined that I would walk out what I had confessed.

Healing Begins

I can't tell you the date my bright and glorious beginning started; but one day I went into my office, looked at Omar's photo, read my daily confession, and smiled. I knew then that I had been healed from the hold that Omar's death and Brian's sentence had on me. It was a triumphant day, and I rejoiced, knowing I did not have to remain a victim forever. As Jesus said in John 8:32, "You will know the truth, and the truth will make you free."

Don't get me wrong. Scars remain in my heart as a reminder of how much I love and miss my precious son. If you've ever cut yourself deeply, you know what I mean. The wound is gone, but the scar remains. And if you have had a total hip replacement as I have or any other major surgery, you know the scar is noticeable. But, by comparison, you also know that it is evidence of the healing that has taken place.

Scars are a Reminder of Jesus

Scars also make me think about when Jesus victoriously arose from the dead after His crucifixion. His body bore evidence of the ferocious torture He had endured. He had wounds on His face, wounds in His hands, wounds in His feet, and wounds in His side.

Those wounds are the reminders of the price He paid for our healing (Isaiah 53:5) and evidence that He has overcome death, hell, and the grave (1 Corinthians 15:55). Jesus is now seated at the right hand of God in heaven, interceding for us as our great High Priest with scars from those same wounds. Therefore, when we suffer, we have the assurance of knowing that He feels our pain and can heal our every hurt.

Blessings from Teardrops

"Heaven and earth may separate us today, but nothing will ever change the fact that you made me a mom."

—*Unknown*

Our Tears Are Not in Vain

*O*ur tears are not in vain. Psalm 126:6 says, "If we sow in tears, we'll reap in joy." Psalm 30:5 tells us, "Weeping may endure for a night, but joy comes in the morning." Singer Richard Smallwood adds, "Tears are for cleansing and release; God created them to give us relief." Singer Renee Bondi says, "Sometimes blessings come through teardrops."

I'm a living witness that tears give relief. I cry periodically 25 years after Omar's death and will continue to shed tears when I think of Him. All that said, I can testify with great conviction that joy does come, and blessings can come from teardrops. My blessings could consume this entire book, so I'll only share a few of them with you.

End Murder Campaign

I started a letter-writing campaign to do what I could to end senseless killings of innocent victims and to ensure that Omar's death was not in vain. I wrote to the President of the United States, United States Congress, Texas Governor, Texas Congress, and crime watch organizations. I also wrote to news stations and every talk show host I could think of—including Jerry Springer—asking for a forum to discuss the senseless murders of our children. I received correspondence back from them but was not allowed to talk. Finally, my friend Sandy asked me to speak on a cable channel about Omar's death and the murders of our children.

National Crime Victim's Week- April 19, 1997

I was the keynote speaker for Parents of Murdered Children. My subject was *"Who's Going to Ring the Bell?"* In my speech, I referred to the song, "If I had a bell, I'd ring it in the morning...." to emphasize that we each have a bell to ring about the crime impacting our brothers and our sisters all over this land. I spoke about four people: Everybody, Somebody, Anybody, and Nobody:

There was an important job to be done, and Everybody was asked to do it. Everybody was sure Somebody would do it. Anybody could have done it, but Nobody did it. Somebody got angry about that because it was Everybody's job. Everybody thought Anybody could do it, but Nobody realized that Everybody wouldn't do it. It ended up that Everybody blamed Somebody when Nobody did what Anybody could have done.[28] I asked what we would do differently, for we all have a part in curbing crime and the terrible sorrow that results.

Letters to Mothers Who Have Lost Children

Shortly after Omar's death, I started writing letters to mothers who had lost children to encourage and strengthen them in their grief journey. By the grace of God, I've written hundreds of letters.

On June 27, 1997, I wrote the first letter to my sister Martha's friend whose son was killed by a drunken driver on June 18, 1997, Omar's first birthday in heaven.

Omar Jamal Aycox Foundation

One of the most note-worthy blessings I have is the Omar Jamal Aycox Foundation (OJAF). It is a non-profit foundation that Joel and I established in Omar's honor a few months after his death. The foundation promotes Omar's legacy of love of God, service to the community, and pursuit of academic excellence. In addition, many sponsors help me award scholarships in Omar's memory to empower young people with the resources necessary to achieve spiritual development and personal success. The foundation has also actively supported many humanitarian causes.

Prayer & Praise Explosion

I mentioned this event a couple of times already. The Explosion was held on Saturday, January 24, 1998. The purpose of the Explosion was to dedicate OJAF, praise and thank God for blessing us to make it through the first year after Omar's death, and help persons who have lost loved ones cope with their grief. We also thanked and presented Special Recognition awards to the law enforcement officers who apprehended Brian Gonzales and Jason Garcia, and to the prosecutors who prosecuted the case. In addition, the Senate of the State of Texas issued two proclamations: No. 850 and No. 861 in honor of Omar. Three hundred people attended the celebration.

The theme for the dedication was "A New Beginning." Below is the full text of my Dedication Message:

Giving honor to God, our Creator, and Sustainer; to Jesus Christ, our Redeemer, Lord, Savior, and only Potentate; and to the Holy Spirit, our Sanctifier, Teacher, Leader, and Comforter. Peace be unto you.

This Praise & Prayer Explosion is dedicated to God; for God and God alone is worthy of the honor and the praise. It is not about Omar. It is not about us. It is not about you. It is about God. God gave us a vision following Omar's death. That vision was to orchestrate an Explosion to praise Him for His abundant grace and mercy—despite the over- whelming trial we were going through. It was also to pray that God would heal our land, for the effectual, fervent prayer of a righteous man avails much. We thank God for counting us worthy to be recipients of the vision, and for allowing us to fulfill the vision through the Omar Jamal Aycox Foundation. We also thank God for each of you, for had not the Holy Spirit put in on your heart to attend the Explosion, and to support the Foundation with your gen- erous contributions, we would not be here tonight. To God be the glory for the things He has done!

Orchestrating the Explosion was not an easy task. We know the Bible tells us in 1st Thessalonians 5:18, "In everything give thanks, for this is the will of God in Christ Jesus con- cerning you." However, when Omar was murdered at 22 years of age, we found little for which to give thanks, for we found ourselves immediately plunged into the pits of Sorrow Valley. To us, Sorrow Valley is a place of shattered dreams and rivers of tears. It is a place of engulfing quick- sand, a place where God deserts you, and leaves you to fend for yourself, a place of unanswered prayers and ques- tions, a place devoid of praise, and a place where you lose your song. Some of you may have spent time in Sorrow Valley in years or months past, some may be in Sorrow Valley now; some will be in Sorrow Valley before 1998 ends. Each one of us will spend time in Sorrow Valley before we go home to be with the Lord.

128

Contrary to our belief, we found out that Sorrow Valley does not have to be a place of hopelessness and helplessness, but a haven of healing. For, in Sorrow Valley God became more real to us than ever before. We found out that God had not lost one iota of His power. He is the same yesterday, today, and forever, and is a right now God. One on whom we could cast all our cares. One who knew how much we could bear. One who understood and felt our pain. One who was a God of restoration—able to restore what the enemy had taken away. One who was able to put together the pieces. One who could do exceedingly abundantly above that which we could ask or think. And by God's power, we found ourselves rising above our state of despair, despondency, and desperation, and tenderly lifted out of Sorrow Valley.

Please don't misunderstand what we are saying. We have a multitude of unanswered questions, and the tears flow when we think of Omar. They will flow until we die; for we loved Omar more than our own lives. But we have the blessed assurance of knowing, despite any turmoil we may face, God is still in control, and is able to deliver us out of any situation. We have the assurance of knowing that one day God will unravel the tapestry of time and all our questions will be answered—for now we see through a glass darkly, but then face to face.

As we continue into 1998, let us seek to do our Father's will. We pray that 1998 will be a year of rededicating our lives to God, and that we will stay focused on the task He has set before us, for the suffering of this present time cannot be compared to the glory that will be revealed in us. When fiery trials come our way, let us trust in God as our ultimate sense of power, and put on the garment of praise for the spirit of heaviness. Greater is He who is within you than he who is in the world!

These words are valid 24 years after I wrote them. Therefore, I do not want to add to or subtract from them.

Savoring Memories

"As long as I live, as long as I breathe, with every beat of my heart, you will not be forgotten. This I promise you."

—Angela Miller

Memories Won't Fade

*M*any parents fear that memories of their deceased child will fade with time. Memories never die. A parent is always a parent. Our children continue to live in our hearts and will forever be a part of our existence. Starting a set of rituals or traditions to remember the joy our children brought to our lives can help keep their memory alive.

In the chapter titled *Midnight Train to Georgia*, I wrote of an encounter I had with a young man in the Atlanta airport on my way home after sending Omar's belongings back to Texas. He told me to look for Omar in my daily encounters.

I took his words to heart and began to look for Omar wherever I went. Honestly, I didn't "see" him often, but that didn't stop my search for reminders. I thought you might be interested in knowing what I'm doing to commemorate Omar's life, in addition to the

Foundation and writing letters. You may want to adopt some of them to supplement your list of rituals or traditions that you are doing to keep your child's memory alive.

Display Case of Memories

The display case is a treasured collection of articles in Omar's former bedroom that remind me of him. Included in the case is The figurine of a young male angel with a dog that I referred to in *Coping with the Holidays,* Goofy with a hole in the sole of his shoe, a clown holding a gigantic fish, Sleepy of the seven dwarfs, a young man playing basketball, an owl, and a bowling trophy. The case also contains Omar's Morehouse class ring, yearbook, and the wallet in his pocket when he died. In addition, I have a display case of porcelain figurines in my dining room that reminds me of Omar.

Plaques

Omar's name is on a Parents of Murdered Children (POMC) plaque in the Harris County Criminal Courthouse, Houston, TX. His name is also on POMC Headquarters Wall in Cincinnati, OH, Panel 20.

Eternal Candle

This is a candle that I purchased from Parents of Murdered Children the year after Omar died. It has burned brightly for 25 years and has no sign of ever going out.

Shrimp, Fries, Salad, Cheesecake

This was Omar's favorite meal. My family and I celebrate his birth and death dates by eating his favorite meal. Red Lobster was his favorite restaurant, and I always try to get a meal there, if possible.

Omar Aycox Endowed Scholarship Fund at Morehouse College

AMC Theaters donated $25,000 in Omar's memory.

The Jackson Family Summit

For several years following Omar's death, my siblings and I held annual family summits to honor Omar and other members of our family who died. At the summit, each member would talk about their accomplishments and challenges during the year. Before the summit, members of our family would vote for the family member of the year. I received the award in 2000. Our goal is to relaunch the forum soon.

A Multitude of Other Ways

There's a multitude of other ways you can savor your child's memory. Below are some unique ways Elaine Stillwell suggests for keeping memories of your child alive:

- Choose meaningful items from your child's life and place them in a prominent place in your home to share stories with visitors (one woman purchased a trunk and put it in her living room).
- Select a few favorite photos and frame them.
- Design screensavers for your computer with your child's photo.
- Spend time looking over cards your child made or bought for you over the years.
- Design vanity license plates or bumper stickers that remind you of your child.
- Offer your child's story on a website bereaved parents have set up.
- Share memories of your child via special Internet chat rooms.
- Design address labels with your child's picture.
- Wear a necklace with your child's picture hanging from it, or a costume pin with your child's photo.
- Establish scholarships at the school your child attended.

- Donate visual gifts (one family funded the refurbishing of a classroom as a mock courtroom for social studies and justice programs).
- Send out a monthly newsletter that focuses specifically on parents who have lost their child or children.
- Share your child's love through random acts of kindness (holding a door, helping someone, picking up a dinner check for an elderly person sitting alone in a restaurant, and others). Always accompany such gestures with a little card that states something like "Act of Kindness in Memory of..." with your child's name and date of birth and death printed on it.[29]

AFTER THIS

After This

"The song is ended, but the melody lingers on..."
— Irving Berlin

We Dance

Tom Zuba says we dance between two worlds when our loved ones die.[30] For me, those worlds are earth and heaven. Although it's been 25 years since Omar's death at the time of this writing, a day doesn't go by that I don't think of him. I've learned to say, "My son is in heaven" without crying. But I also have a locked door in my heart that will not open until we dance together again. I'm sure many of you reading this book feel the same way about your beloved child.

Dancing with our children is not a pipe dream. From God's perspective, their lives aren't lost, for life isn't lost to the One who can restore it. Those who have not lost a child but have experienced other crushing losses can also dance.

Place Our Trust In God

In the interim, like me, some of you may have withdrawn from God. I pray that my story will help you find your way to reconnect with Him, whatever the reason.

Reconnecting with God will not happen overnight, nor should you expect it to happen that quickly. But, no matter how long it takes, as your fellow traveler through the valley of the shadow of death, let me assure you that it can happen. God did it for me, and He will do it for you.

As you read in my story, reconnecting with God starts with having a deeper trust in Him. The more we draw closer to God, the more we trust Him. Trust is also a continuum. The closer we get to God, the more our faith is strengthened. The stronger our belief, the easier it is to conclude, as my son Jay always reminds me, "God is good."

Some days you can see the positive aspect of your situation. Some days you will cry. Some days you will want to get in bed, pull up the covers and never come out again. Some days you will look around and see nothing but the walls around you. Some days you may have thoughts of suicide wanting to be with your child. Some days you will want to raise your fist to heaven and shout, "Why?" Some days there will be no words to express the seemingly inexpressible.

That is because we trust a God who allows hurt, for we live in a broken world where broken things happen. But we also trust a God who uses hurt for good, even when—especially when—life doesn't make sense. And we can trust in His promises.

God never promised to spare us from heartache or heartbreak. He didn't even promise that our child would not die before us. But He did promise that He would never leave us or forsake us (Hebrews 13:5). He promised that nothing would separate us from His love (Romans 8:37-39). He promised that He had put our tears in His bottle (Psalm 56:8) and promised that one day He was going to wipe away every tear from our eyes (Revelation 7:17). These are great promises, as are all the other promises I've referred to in my book. We can cling to them with much gratitude for the rest of our lives.

The Most Crucial Step

The most crucial step in reconnecting with God is a personal relationship with our Lord and Savior, Jesus Christ. That is the only way we can have the assurance of dancing with our children and other loved ones in heaven. As David said in 2 Samuel 12:23, after his child died, they cannot come to us, but we can go to them.

If you have never trusted Jesus as your Savior and want the assurance of eternal life, please pray this prayer with me right now:

God, I've sinned; I'm sorry; forgive me. I believe Jesus is your Son, and I want to trust Him as my Savior. I accept His work and death on the cross as sufficient payment for my sins and invite Him to come into my heart and take control of my life. Through faith in Jesus, I have eternal life. Please give me the wisdom and determination to walk in the center of Your will. In Jesus' name, I pray. Amen.

In Closing

Thank you again for reading my book. My story isn't over; in many ways, it's just beginning. Your story isn't over either. I ask God to give you comfort when you are bereaved, strength when you are weary, hope when your hope is gone, and to meet you in the silence.

Until We All Get to Heaven

The Lord bless you and keep you; the Lord make His face shine on you and be gracious to you; the Lord lift His countenance upon you and give you peace.

—Numbers 6:24-26

I send you my love,
Sena

PHOTO ALBUM

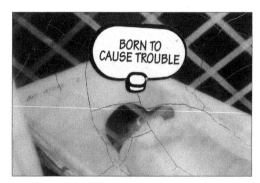

The "Prince" is born

With cousin Icie

With big brother, Jay

First Christmas

Elementary school photo

Family time with Jay and Mom

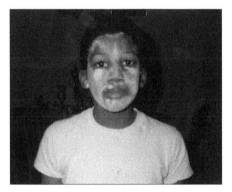

Measles and calamine lotion

All dressed up for Easter

Before Freres Jacques "performance"

**With Grandmom,
Jay, and Mom**

**With legendary saxophonist the late
Dr. Vernard Johnson**

Inducted into the Junior Honor Society—
Jr. high school

Football trophy- Jr. high school

Academic achievement award- high school

With Mom after receiving an academic
achievement award

With Bo, the dog who
doesn't like a leash

On an alligator tour
in Louisiana

**With Olivia at high
school prom**

**Another academic achievement
award—high school**

**High school
graduation photo**

Receiving high school diploma

With Aunt Marian and friend on high school graduation day

Celebrating his 18th birthday

Spending brother time with Jay

Spending more brother time with Jay

Morehouse College orientation

Picture sent to Omar of mother
washing baby

Sending Mom greetings from Morehouse

May 1996 Morehouse graduation class
(Omar is on the front row, right side)

"Official" Morehouse
graduation photo

Last photo taken at Morehouse

Celebrating graduation day with friends

AMC Theater Manager photo

Joel, Sena & Jay present
appreciation plaques at the Omar
Jamal Aycox Foundation (OJAF)
Praise & Prayer Explosion

Sena and Jay praising God for His
goodness and mercy

Jay and cousins remembering Omar
at the Jackson Family Summit

APPENDIX A
LIFELINES

Stretcher-Bearers

"Friendship improves happiness, and abates misery, by doubling our joys, and dividing our grief."

— *Marcus Tullius Cicero*

*M*ark 2:1-12 records a beautiful story of how four of a lame man's friends put him on a stretcher and lowered him through a roof so Jesus could heal him. I call these men stretcher-bearers—friends who carry you. Stretcher-bearers aren't pallbearers. They carry the living; pallbearers carry the dead. We all need stretcher-bearers after the death of our child or a catastrophic loss. Proverbs 17:17 tells us that brothers are born for the day of adversity.

One of the most remarkable manifestations of God's love for me was the stretcher-bearers He put in my life to carry me through my grief after Omar's death. I mentioned some of them on the Acknowledgment page of my book. But I wanted to discuss the importance of stretcher-bearers more fully in this Appendix because they are lifelines. I couldn't have made it without my stretcher-bearers. I was not lame physically, but I was lame emotionally and spiritually. Sometimes I felt like the living dead.

My stretcher-bearers surrounded me and were quick to extend their support, sympathy, and empathy and help me any way they could. They also gave me their strength when I couldn't find it within myself. Additionally, they gave me time for my mind to slow down and my heart to beat.

My biggest regret about my stretcher-bearers was that I kept things hidden from them when I was going through my struggles. That was dangerous and caused me to take too long to go through the grief process. If I had shared my feelings with my stretcher-bearers, they could have said, "I'm dragging you up on this rooftop and am taking you to Jesus so He can heal you!"

Your stretcher-bearers will do the same for you. I pray that you will surround yourself with them and open your heart to them.

Forgiveness

"*Forgiveness isn't approving what happened. It's choosing to rise above it.*"

—*Robin Sharma*

*F*orgiveness is a lifeline. I wrote about forgiveness in *Are You Kidding Me?* and told you how hard it was for me to forgive the men responsible for Omar's death. Some of you reading this book who have had a child or loved one killed or have had other disastrous losses caused by others may feel as I did. So, I'd like to pause for a moment and discuss forgiveness again, as this topic is so essential to healing.

Forgiveness helps the forgiver. Someone said, "Unforgiveness is like drinking poison and thinking it is going to hurt someone else."

Gerald Sittser adds to this truth:

> *The real problem, however, is not revenge, but the unforgiving heart behind the revenge. Unforgiveness is like a fire that smolders in the belly, like smoke that smothers the soul. It is destructive because it is insidious. Occasionally it flares up in the form of bitter denunciation and explosions of rage. But most of the time, it is content to stay*

low to the ground, where it goes unnoticed, quietly doing its deadly work.[31]

Bob Gass tells us that unforgiveness can prevent us from moving forward:

You can't enter into the next season of your life with integrity if you don't exit this season right...Close it with forgiveness. Bitterness will poison your attitude and your memories. It'll destroy you. Give to God those who have hurt you and let Him do the correcting—you're not qualified.[32]

And we have God's Word that He will correct. God said, "Vengeance is Mine, I will repay" (Hebrews 10:30). Vengeance is not revenge. The difference is love, grace, mercy, and justice.

After you forgive, don't expect to forget because you can't. How could you ever forget your child's murder or crippling loss, no matter what the circumstance? Still, I want to forgive, and I won't forgive are not the same thing.

Finally, there is no true forgiveness without the work of the Holy Spirit, so please let Him lead you to the path of forgiveness if you haven't already found it.

My prayer is that you will choose forgiveness.

Stages of Grief

"Grief, I've learned, is really just love. It's all the love you want to give but cannot. All that unspent love gathers up in the corners of your eyes, the lump in your throat, and in that hollow part of your chest. Grief is just love with no place to go."

— *Jamie Anderson*

*K*nowing the stages of grief can be a lifeline to you after the death of your child or other loved one. It was to me. The notion that we go through stages of grief after losing a loved one came from Elizabeth Kübler-Ross. In her view, there are five distinct stages of grief: denial, anger, bargaining, depression, and acceptance, and we progress through them one step at a time.

Jodi Clarke describes the stages this way:[33]

Stage 1: Denial
Denial helps us minimize the overwhelming pain of loss. As we process the reality of our loss, we are also trying to survive emotional pain. It can be hard to believe we have lost an important person in our lives, especially when we may have just spoken with this person the previous week or even the previous day.

Stage 2: Anger
It is common to experience anger after the loss of a loved one. We're trying to adjust to a new reality, and we are likely experiencing extreme emotion and discomfort. There is so much to process that anger may feel like it allows us an emotional outlet.

Stage 3: Bargaining
When coping with loss, it isn't unusual to feel so desperate that you are willing to do almost anything to alleviate or minimize the pain. Losing a loved one can cause us to consider any way we can to avoid the current pain or the pain we are anticipating from loss.

Stage 4: Depression
There comes a time when our imaginations calm down and we slowly start to look at the reality of our present situation. Bargaining no longer feels like an option and we are faced with what is happening. We start to feel the loss of our loved one more abundantly. As our panic begins to subside, the emotional fog begins to clear, and the loss feels more present and unavoidable

Stage 5: Acceptance
When we come to a place of acceptance, it is not that we no longer feel the pain of loss. However, we are no longer resisting the reality of our situation, and we are not struggling to make it something different. Sadness and regret can still be present in this phase, but the emotional survival tactics of denial, bargaining, and anger are less likely to be present.

Familiarity with these stages of grief helped me know that I wasn't crazy or unique in how I dealt with Omar's death. I hope it will help you too—whether you're new to grief or have been grieving for years. Nonetheless, a model is good, but one size doesn't fit all. For example, you can't schedule time on your calendar for when you will grieve, and you can't set a timer to determine how long you will suffer or how long you will stay in each stage.

As Ms. Clarke writes,

> *Whatever time it takes for you to move through these stages is perfectly normal. Your pain is unique to you, your relationship to the person you lost is unique, and the emotional processing can feel different to each person. It is acceptable for you to take the time you need and remove any expectation of how you should be performing as you process your grief.*[34]

Furthermore, according to the US Department of Justice:

> *With deaths other than murder, it usually takes 18 to 24 months just to stabilize. It can take much longer when the death was violent. Recovering from the murder of a loved one will take a long time and will not be easy. It will help if you don't expect too much of yourself and others.*[35]

Also, remove any expectation of how others will respond to your grief. Some people will give you the time you need to process your grief and will be empathetic. Others have a timetable for you to grieve. While you are within their schedule, they will listen to you talk about your grief and loss, but your story may get old after a while, and they won't want to hear it. They want you to get on with your life and let them get on with theirs. Some people simply don't like to talk about death or anything associated with it. Some may be uncomfortable when you talk about your child's death because they don't know what to say.

I experienced all these responses when I was grieving Omar's death—especially making people uncomfortable. Sometimes, when I mentioned his name, I felt like I was opening Pandora's box. For that reason, I found myself pacing my grief and my conversations about him. I still do.

Be that as it may, there is one Somebody that will listen to you all day and all night, 24/7. I'm talking about God, of course. He is concerned about you and your grief—no matter what stage.

Counseling

"He that won't be counseled can't be helped."

—Benjamin Franklin

$\mathcal{B}$y God's grace, I didn't have to take medication or seek counseling or psychotherapy to cope with Omar's death, but everyone is different. If you do, there is no reason to feel guilty or ashamed. On the contrary, it can be a lifeline. So, lovingly pray and ask God to direct you to the proper source. If needed, here is some information from Dr. Amanda Spencer that I included in my book, *I'm Sleeping With the Pastor!!!,* that may help you to make a better decision:[36]

Therapist

You talk with a therapist to help you through situations and help you gain or improve coping skills. One of the main questions a therapist will ask is, "What has to change to make you feel better about this situation?" If you are looking for a therapist, ask about his/her clinical perspectives and skillsets.

Types of Therapists

- *Licensed Clinical Social Worker (LCSW).* They practice independently and provide counseling. They have a master's degree in social work and are licensed to practice as a therapist.

- *Licensed Professional Counselor (LPC).* They have a master's degree in counseling and can practice as a therapist.
- *Licensed Marriage Family Therapist (LMFT).* They focus on family and marriage counseling.
- *Licensed Chemical Dependency Counselor (LCDC).* Chemical dependent issues.
- *Psychologists (Ph. D, or Psy.D); Doctor in Psychology.* They have a license and can perform therapy and make psychological assessments and diagnoses. In some states, they can give medication.
- *Psychiatrists.* They have a medical degree and can give medication and treat disorders. Psychiatric treatment will include medication intervention and a psychologist to follow up and provide psychotherapy.

Dr. Spencer recommends going to your doctor first if you have physical symptoms to ensure nothing is going on medically. If the symptoms are not relieving themselves, and you know that other things are going on, you may want to seek counseling. You may want to start with an LPC or LCSW. Ask about their theoretical orientation (what they specialize in). If your problem is above their scope, they will refer you to a psychologist.

Costs

Many insurance plans have mental health benefits that pay for some of these services or co-pays that will reimburse you. Check your mental health benefits. Samaritan Counseling Centers typically provide therapy free or on a sliding scale.

Some colleges and universities have psychological services when you can't afford to pay, so check with schools in your area.

Prayers

"Any concern too small to be turned into a prayer is too small to be made into a burden."

—Corrie ten Boom

Parent's Prayer for Loss of a Child

*L*oving Father, grant me peace, for I am full of fear and anxiety. I rest in your warm embrace, for I know that you will never let me go. Cover me with your wings of love and grant my family and me the peace that surpasses all understanding during this trying moment as we mourn the loss of our child.[37]

Prayer for Comfort

Dear God, I bring every grieving parent into your throne of grace. Lord, they are going through a lot of pain after the loss of their children. It is not an easy thing for a parent to bury their child. Father, comfort them. Help them to continue being faithful to you even through the pain. Lavish them with your love and fill the void left in their hearts with your unconditional love. In Jesus' powerful name, I believe and pray. Amen.[38]

Prayer for a Grieving Family after a Tragedy

Abba Father, You hold time within your hands and see it all, from beginning to end. Please keep and carry these precious people in their sadness and loss. Cover them with your great wings of love, give their weary hearts rest, and their minds sound sleep. Lord, lift their eyes so that they may catch a glimpse of eternity and be comforted by the promise of heaven. We ask all this in the precious name of Jesus. Amen.[39]

Prayer for First Responders

Almighty God, you lend your strength to all those who are there for us in times of crisis, fear, and hurt. You give courage to the first responders who continue to do this important work they are called to do, looking beyond the risk for the sake of those who need your help and protection. We give you thanks for the many ways they give of themselves, their skills, knowledge, and help in troubling times. Protect them, O Lord. Extend your shielding hand over them and comfort their hearts when they are tired and heartbroken.

God, we also lift prayers of thanksgiving and comfort for the families of first responders and all who support them. Give them hope and courage. Surround them with your loving presence and give them peace when their loved ones run toward uncertainty. All this, we pray in your name. Amen.[40]

Prayer for Our Justice System

Almighty God, you are a God of justice and righteousness. The prophet Amos says, "may justice roll down like a river, and righteousness like a never-failing stream." We pray for the justice system in our country. May judges, legislators, and law enforcement work with community leaders and advocates to end oppression and exploitation, together bringing justice to our city and our nation.[41]

Comforting Scriptures

"The more you read the Bible, the more you'll love the Author."

—Anna Sasine

The greatest consolation we can find after the death of our child, other loved ones, or any drastic loss is God's Word. Therefore, I pray the Scriptures I have listed throughout my book, and those below will comfort you in your time of sorrow. All Scriptures are from the New King James Version Bible, except where noted:

Job 2:10b
Shall we indeed accept good from God, and shall not accept adversity?

Job 14:5 (NLT)
You have decided the length of our lives. You know how many months we will live, and we are not given a minute longer.

Psalm 23:1
The Lord is my shepherd; I shall not want.

Psalm 34:18-19

The Lord is near to those who have a broken heart, And saves such as have a contrite spirit. Many are the afflictions of the righteous, But the Lord delivers him out of them all.

Psalm 116:15

Precious in the sight of the Lord Is the death of His saints.

Psalm 145:17-18

The Lord is righteous in all His ways, Gracious in all His works. The Lord is near to all who call upon Him, to all who call upon Him in truth.

Psalm 147:3

He heals the brokenhearted and binds up their wounds.

Isaiah 25:4

For You have been a strength to the poor, A strength to the needy in his distress, A refuge from the storm, a shade from the heat.

Isaiah 25:8

He will swallow up death forever, And the Lord God will wipe away tears from all faces.

Isaiah 40:28-31

Have you not known? Have you not heard? The everlasting God, the Lord, The Creator of the ends of the earth, neither faints nor is weary...

Isaiah 41:10

Fear not, for I am with you; Be not dismayed, for I am your God. I will strengthen you, Yes, I will help you, I will uphold you with My righteous right hand.

Isaiah 43:2

When you pass through the waters, I will be with you.

Isaiah 54:17
No weapon formed against you shall prosper.

Isaiah 57:1-2 (NLT)
Good people pass away; the godly often die before their time. But no one seems to care or wonder why. No one seems to understand that God is protecting them from the evil to come. For those who follow godly paths will rest in peace when they die.

Jeremiah 17:7-8 (NLT)
But blessed are those who trust in the Lord and have made the Lord their hope and confidence.

Jeremiah 29:11
For I know the thoughts that I think toward you, says the Lord, thoughts of peace and not of evil, to give you a future and a hope.

Matthew 5:4
Blessed are those who mourn, for they shall be comforted.

Matthew 18:14
Even so it is not the will of your Father who is in heaven that one of these little ones should perish.

John 3:16
For God so loved the world that He gave His only begotten Son, that whoever believes in Him should not perish but have everlasting life.

John 11:25
Jesus said to her, "I am the resurrection and the life. "

John 14:1
Let not your heart be troubled; you believe in God, believe also in Me.

Romans 8:38-39 (NLT)

I am convinced that nothing can ever separate us from God's love. Neither death nor life, neither angels nor demons, neither our fears for today nor our worries about tomorrow—not even the powers of hell can separate us from God's love. No power in the sky above or in the earth below—indeed, nothing in all creation will ever be able to separate us from the love of God that is revealed in Christ Jesus our Lord.

Romans 14:8

For if we live, we live to the Lord; and if we die, we die to the Lord. Therefore, whether we live or die, we are the Lord's.

1 Corinthians 15:55

"O Death, where is your sting? O Hades, where is your victory?"

2 Corinthians 1:3-4

Blessed be the God and Father of our Lord Jesus Christ, the Father of mercies and God of all comfort, who comforts us in all our tribulation, that we may be able to comfort those who are in any trouble, with the comfort with which we ourselves are comforted by God.

2 Corinthians 4:17

For our light affliction, which is but for a moment, is working for us a far more exceeding and eternal weight of glory.

1 Thessalonians 4:13

But I do not want you to be ignorant, brethren, concerning those who have fallen asleep, lest you sorrow as others who have no hope.

Revelation 21:1-27

Now I saw a new heaven and a new earth, for the first heaven and the first earth had passed away...

APPENDIX B
OTHER RESOURCES

The Wrong Things People Say

"Easy for you to say 'God needed another angel' since He didn't ask for yours."

–Angela Miller

$\mathcal{S}$ome of your well-meaning friends and acquaintances will say things that unintentionally cause you more grief when they try to comfort you. Instead of helping you, they are like the "worthless physicians" Job called his friends in Job 13:4 when they wanted to get him to repent of the wrongdoing they thought caused Job's loss of everything he had—including his children. Unfortunately, you may already have had encounters with some of them.

I didn't call any of my friends "worthless physicians," but some of the things they said were hurtful. One stands out in my mind: A friend asked me if I'd rather that my son Jay be murdered instead of Omar. I couldn't tell her what I was thinking, but I wanted to strangle her! I love Jay as much as I love Omar. Would any mother in her right mind want to trade one of her children for another? That's beyond crazy! At the same time, I knew this person cared for me. She just didn't know what to say.

Sandy Peckinpah gives us good advice on what to do when the wrong things come out of people's mouths:

- **Very simply, just breathe** and know their intention is to help you, not to harm you.
- **Allow feelings of love to fill the awkward space**. Hard to imagine! Just as if it was their loss.
- **Respond by saying,** "Thank You." Now is not the time to struggle with relationships nor is it the time to teach them how wrong they are.
- **A hug gives a physical connection of understanding**. If you are comfortable, offer one.
- **Again...Just breathe.**[42]

Supporting the Bereaved

"Some people don't realize how the loss of a child changes you. They expect u to be the same though u will never be."

–Nanci Luna

There are many helpful things you can do to support the bereaved after the death of their child.

Dr. Catherine Sanders writes:

Don't ask the grieving person what you can do, just do it. The bereaved parent will not be able to think what needs to be done. Carry your tasks through quietly:

1. Offer to write or call out-of-town friends who haven't heard about the death yet.
2. Bring over meals or special dishes. Your thoughtfulness in preparing something will be deeply appreciated.
3. Go to the grocery store for the bereaved family.
4. Offer to take care of small children.
5. Answer the phone.
6. Wash the car and fill it with gas.

7. House-sit.
8. Vacuum and clean the house.
9. Wash towels and bed linens or anything else that needs it.
10. Mow the grass or rake leaves.
11. Send a sympathy letter and include any memories you have of the child. Emotionally, that child is still alive to the parents and reminders of special remembrances are tremendously important for them.

After the funeral:

1. Offer to address thank-you cards.
2. Invite the bereaved parents to have coffee, tea.
3. Take them to breakfast or lunch.
4. Offer to go to the cemetery with them.
5. Take a small flowering plant or bouquet.
6. Help sort the child's belongings.
7. Taxi the children to lessons.
8. Continue to do the things mentioned in the first list.
9. Continue phoning or visiting but always, always, arrange a visit ahead of time.
10. Invite them to go on short junkets. Keep outings short and simple because the strength of those in grief is tenuous.[43]

For Victims
of Crime

"For too long, the victims of crime have been the forgotten persons of our criminal justice system."

—*Ronald Reagan*

*P*articipating in the criminal justice process was necessary for my healing and closure. Below is a list of things I found helpful:

1. Familiarize yourself with criminal proceedings.
2. Get involved in all phases of the trial.
3. Have a sound support system.
4. Prepare a Victim's Impact Statement.
5. Be cooperative with the Prosecutor.
6. Talk with others who have gone through a similar situation.
7. Provide photos of your loved one or any information you feel will help to ensure the perpetrator is given a sentence commensurate with the crime.
8. Make a copy of the perpetrator's arrest record and convictions to get to know something about the perpetrator before going to court.

9. Be prompt at the trial.
10. Sit on the front row in the courtroom, if possible.
11. Take notes, if possible.
12. Be cordial with the perpetrator's family, but not too friendly.
13. When the trial is over, send a letter to the Prosecutors, thanking them for their efforts in prosecuting your loved one's murder or other crime.
14. Pray, pray, pray!

Self-Help
Organizations

"Be strong enough to stand alone, smart enough to know when you
need help, and brave enough to ask for it."

—Ziad K. Abdelnour

The Compassionate Friends (TCF)
48660 Pontiac Trail
#930808
Wixom, MI 48393
(877) 969-0010
Provides volunteer self-help for bereaved parents.

National Organization for Victim Assistance (NOVA)
510 King Street, Suite 424
Alexandria, VA 22314
(703) 535-6682
Advocates for victims of crime by connecting them with services
and resources.

Parents of Murdered Children (POMC)
635 W. 7th Street, Suite 104
Cincinnati, OH 45023
(513) 721-5683
Puts families who have experienced the death of a murdered child
in touch with one another.

Victims of Crime and Leniency (VOCAL)
PO Box 4449
Montgomery, AL 36103
(800) 239-3219
Keeps victims of crime informed of issues and educates the public
of the injustices in the judicial system.

American Justice Institute
530 Bercut Drive
Sacramento, CA 95811
(Phone number is not listed)
Conducts basic research and surveys; educates its members and
the public about crime and delinquency problems and practical
solutions.

American Sudden Infant Death Syndrome Institute
528 Raven Way
Naples, FL 34110
(239) 431-5425
Helps parents deal with the shock and grief of losing their
babies to SIDS.

The Candlelighters Childhood Cancer Family Alliance
121919 Southwest Freeway, Suite 100
Stafford, TX 77477
(713) 270-4700
Supports parents of children who have or who have had cancer.

Mothers Against Drunk Driving (MADD)
511 E. John Carpenter Freeway
Irving, TX 75062
(877) 275-6233
Educates the public about the dangers of drunk driving.

Samaritans Grief Support Service
41 West Street, 4th Floor
Boston, MA 02111
(617) 536-2460
Provides self-help support for survivors of suicide victims.

The American Association of Pastoral Counselors
1025 Thomas Jefferson St., NW, Ste 700W
Washington, DC 20007
(800) 273-8255
Equips faith communities to support suicide prevention.

APPENDIX C
Suggestions for Further Reading

Suggestions for Further Reading

Here's a list of my favorite books on working through grief:

Death of a Child

Elizabeth B. Brown, *Surviving the Loss of a Child: Support for Grieving Parents* (Grand Rapids: Baker Publishing Group, published by Revell, 2010).

Ann K. Finkbeiner, *After the Death of a Child: Living With Loss Through the Tears* (Baltimore: The John Hopkins University Press, 1996).

Brook Noll, and Pamela D. Blair, Ph.D. *I Wasn't Ready to Say Goodbye: Surviving, Coping, & Healthy Healing after the Sudden Death of a Loved One* (Naperville: Sourcebooks, Inc., 2008).

Karen F. Norton, *Mom God's Got This: Jamie's Story* (Mustang: Tate Publishing and Enterprises, LLC, 2016).

Sandy Peckinah, *How to Survive the Worst That Can Happen: A Parent's Step by Step Guide to Healing After the Loss of a Child* (Bloomington: Balboa Press, 2014).

Catherine M. Sanders, Ph.D., *How to Survive the Loss of a Child: Filling the Emptiness and Rebuilding Your Life* (Rocklin: Prima Publishing, 1992).

Norma Sawyers-Kurz, *The Grieving Parent's Book of Hope: How to Survive the Loss of Your Child* (Bolivar: 2014).

Elaine E. Stillwell, *The Death of a Child: Reflections for Grieving Parents* (Skokie: ACTA Publications, 2004).

Mary A. White, *Harsh Grief Gentle Hope* (Colorado Springs: Navpress, 1995).

Grief Recovery

Jehu Thomas Burton, *Trusting God Through Tears: A Story to Encourage* (Grand Rapids: Baker Books, 2000).

Carol L. Fitzpatrick, *A Time to Grieve: Help and Hope from the Bible* (Uhrichsville: Barbour and Company, Inc, date unknown).

Earl A. Grollman, *What Helped Me When My Loved One Died* (Boston: Beacon Press, 1981).

John W. James and Russell Friedman, *The Grief Recovery Handbook, 20th Anniversary Expanded Edition: The Action Program for Moving Beyond Death, Divorce, and Other Losses including Health, Career and Faith* (New York: Harper-Collins, 2009).

Elizabeth Kübler-Ross, *On Death and Dying* (New York: The Macmillan Co., 1969).

Ellen Mitchell, *Beyond Tears: living after losing a child* (New York: St. Martin's Griffin, 2009).

Michelle A. Reiss, Ph.D., *Lessons in Loss and Living: Hope and Guidance for Confronting Serious Illness and Grief* (New York: Hyperion, 2010).

Gary Roe, *Please Be Patient, I'm Grieving: How to Care For and Support the Grieving Heart* (Gary Roe: 2016).

Granger E. Westberg, *Good Grief: 50th Anniversary Edition* (Minneapolis: Fortress Press, 2011).

Alice J. Wisler, *Getting Out of Bed in the Morning: Reflections of Comfort in Heartache* (Abilene: Leafwood Publishers, 2013).

Tom Zuba, *Permission to Mourn: A New Way to Do Grief* (Rockford: Bish Press, 2015).

Spiritual Recovery

Dr. James Dobson, *Holding on to Your Faith: Even...When God Doesn't Make Sense* (Wheaton: Tyndale House Publishers, Inc., 1993).

Miriam and Stuart Bundy, *Restoring The Soul: Experiencing God's Grace in Time of Crisis* (Chicago: Moody Press, 1999).

Ken Gire, *The North Face of God: Hope for the Times When God Seems Indifferent* (Wheaton: Tyndale House Publishers, Inc., 2005).

Dan Harrison, *Strongest in the Broken Places: A Story of Spiritual Recovery* (Downers Grove: InterVarsity Press, 1990).

Harold S. Kushner, W*hen Bad Things Happen to Good People* (New York: Avon Press, 1983).

Gerald L. Sittser, *A Grace Disguised: How the Soul Grows Through Loss* (Grand Rapids: Zondervan Publishing House, 1995).

Betty Rollin, *Here's the Bright Side: Of Failure, Fear, Cancer, Divorce, and Other Bum Raps* (New York: Random House, 2007).

Charles Stanley, *How to Handle Adversity* (Nashville: Oliver-Nelson Books, 1989).

Robert Veninga, *A Gift of Hope: How We Survive Our Tragedies* (New York: Ballantine Books, 1985).

Special Issues

Dr. Gloria Horsley, Gloria Dr., and Dr. Heidi Horsley, *Open to Hope: Inspirational Stories for Handling the Holidays After Loss* (Palo Alto: Open to Hope Foundation, 2011).

John W. James and Russell Friedman, with Dr. Leslie Landon Matthews. *When Children Grieve: For Adults to Help Children Deal with Death, Divorce, Pet Loss, Moving, and Other Losses* (New York: Harper, 2001).

Warren Wiersbe and David W. Wiersbe. *Comforting the Bereaved: For Pastors and Others Who Minister* (Chicago: Moody Press, 1985).

ABOUT THE AUTHOR

About the Author

Sena Whitaker, Ph.D., Th.D., D.D., has a fondness for writing down her thoughts. It has resulted in two books, "I'm Sleeping with the Pastor!!!," which she co-authored with her husband, Pastor Earl Whitaker, Sr., and "What Shall We Do With Mom?" a memoir/self-help book about her struggle with caring for her aging mother. She is also an ordained minister, with certifications in expository preaching and Christian counseling; the founding president of Ministers of the Heart, Inc., an Interdenominational Fellowship of Female Ministers and Other Women of God; and the founding president of the Omar Jamal Aycox Foundation, Inc., a tribute to the memory of her son.

Scriptures that guide her life and ministry are Philippians 4:13, "I can do all things through Christ who strengthens me" and Psalm 73:25, "Whom have I in heaven but You? And *there is* none upon earth *that* I desire besides You."

Endnotes

1   Bishop Wheeler Jones, Facebook, October 3, 2016, https://www.facebook.com.

2   Deborah Carr cited in Joshua A. Krisch, *What the Loss of a Child Does to Parents, Psychologically and Biologically,* May 22, 2020. http://www.fatherly.com.

3   The Compassionate Friends, *When Your Child Dies by Homicide, 2017.* https://www.compassionatefrends.org

4   Statistica Research Department, *Society, Crime and Enforcement,* October 1, 2020. http://www.statistica.com.

5   Source unknown.

6   Dr. Richard Seltzer, "Letters to a Young Doctor," cited in Dr. James Dobson, *Holding on to Your Faith even...When God Doesn't Make Sense,* (Wheaton: Tyndale House Publishers, 1993), 10-11.

7   Robert L. Veninga, *A Gift of Hope, How We Survive Our Tragedies,* (New York: Ballantine Books, 1985), 43-57.

8   Dr. David Jeremiah, "The Darkest Hour," *Turning Points Magazine and Devotional,* November 2016, 9.

9   Dr, Sena Whitaker, *I'm Sleeping with the Pastor!!!: Success Kit for Pastors' Wives and those who love us,* (Cypress: EARSEN Publishing Company, 2014), 72.

10 Brook Noll, and Pamela D. Blair, Ph.D. *I Wasn't Ready to Say Goodbye: Surviving, Coping, & Healthy Healing after the Sudden Death of a Loved One* (Naperville: Sourcebooks, Inc., 2008), 41.

11 Jeremiah, "First Ray of Hope," 13.

12 Noll and Blair, *I Wasn't Ready to Say Goodbye: Surviving, Coping, & Healthy Healing after the Sudden Death of a Loved One*, 37.

13 Reverend Kim Hatton and Christina Hollie, eds., "Profile: Dr. Sena Thompson," in Exodus Magazine, August/September 1999, 45.

14 Dr. Charles Stanley, "The Believer's War Room," in *Sermon Notes from In Touch with Dr. Charles Stanley*. https://www.intouch.org.

15 Murray Newman, *Life at the Harris County Criminal Justice Center,"* April 8, 2008. https://murraynewman.com (the post has been deleted).

16 Kenneth W. Osbeck, *Amazing Grace: 366 Hymn stories for personal devotions,* (Grand Rapids: Kregel Publications), August 15.

17 Ken Gire, *The North Face of God: Help for the times when God seems indifferent,* (Wheaton: Tyndale House, 2005), xiv.

18 Wikipedia, *"Mt. Everest,"* https://www.en.m.wikipedia.org.

19 Andrew I. Sutherland, *"Why Are So Many People Dying on Everest?", August 26, 2006. https://www.ncbi.nlm.nih.gov/pmc/articles/PMC1553507/*

20 Jeff Bonaldi, *"14 Fast Facts About Mt. Everest"*, https://www.explorerpassage.com

21 Hairline Fracture: Types, Symptoms, Causes, and Treatment. https://www.healthline.com/health/hairline-fracture.

22 John W. James and Russell Friedman, *The Grief Recovery Handbook, 20ᵗʰ Anniversary Expanded Edition: The Action Program for Moving Beyond Death, Divorce, and Other Losses including Health, Career and Faith,* (New York: Harper-Collins, 2009), 5.

23 Sheila Walsh, "Pray When God Seems Silent" in *Praying Women: How to Pray When You Don't Know What to Say*, Kindle e-book.

24 Miriam and Stuart Bundy, *Restoring the Soul: Experiencing God's Grace in Times of Crisis,* (Chicago: Moody Press, 1999), 96.

25 Airraz. *What Does it Mean to Trust God Wholeheartedly?* January 11, 2021, http://www.Christian.net

26 David Nolte, *"So, What Kind Of Love Is That?"* https://www.sermoncentral.com/sermons/so-what-kind-of-love-is-that-david-nolte-sermon-on-gods-love-236920

27 Bible.org, *"The Righteousness of God"* https://bible.org/seriespage/6-righteousness-god

28 Columbia University in the City of New York, *"Whose Job Is It?"* http://www.columbia.edu/~sss31/rainbow/whose.job.html

29 Elaine E. Stillwell, *The Death of a Child*, (Skokie: ACTA Publishers, 2004), 141-150.

30 Tom Zuba, *Permission to Mourn: A New Way to Do Grief*, (Rockford: Bish Press, 2014), 6.

31 Gerald L. Sittser, *"A Grace Disguised: How the Soul Grows Through Loss"* (Grand Rapids, Michigan: Zondervan Publishing House, 1995), 20.

32 Bob Gass, *"A Fresh Word for Today: 365 Insights For Daily Living."* (Gainesville, FL: Bridge-Logos Publishers, Reprinted 2000), July 24.

33 Jodi Clarke, "The Five Stages of Grief," Updated February 12, 2021). https://www.verywellmind.com

34 Clarke, "The Five Stages of Grief."

35 US Department of Justice, "Coping After A Homicide: A Guide for Family & friends." https://www.coping (justice.gov).

36 Whitaker, 214-216.

37 Traditional and Contemporary Prayers, "Prayer for Loss of Child, Comfort." https://www.lords-prayer-words.com

38 Traditional and Contemporary Prayers.

39 Traditional and Contemporary Prayers.

40 Augsburg University, "A Prayer for...First Responders," (Posted on March 25, 2020). https://www.augsburg.edu.

41 Rackcdn.com, "Prayer for our Justice System," Grace, Justice & Mercy Guide. https://www.c4265878.ssl.cf2.rackcdn.com

42 Sandy Peckinah. *How to Survive the Worst That Can Happen: A Parent's Step by Step Guide to Healing After the Loss of a Child.* Bloomington: Balboa Press, 2014, 42-45

43 Catherine M Sanders, Ph.D., *How to Survive the Loss of a Child: Filling the Emptiness and Rebuilding Your Life.* Rocklin, CA: Prima Publishing, 1992, 223-225.

CPSIA information can be obtained
at www.ICGtesting.com
Printed in the USA
LVHW050453110622
720834LV00003B/5